Dedication

To faithful pioneers who invested their lives in the Sunday School movement—making Bible study available to everyone.

To contemporary heroes—Sunday School directors, teacher, ministers of education, pastors, and others—who carry the light of the gospel today.

To 21st-century leaders who will ensure that people continue to gather to study and apply God's Word.

To my mentor, Jim Neyland, who influenced the establishment of my work as a young minister of education and has encouraged me in every step of my ministry.

To Rose, my lovely wife and dearest friend, who has been used of God to help me to remain focused in my service to the Lord.

To my significant twos: Billy and Brent, my two strong sons who are strong in the Lord; Donna and Allison, my two beautiful daughters-in-law who have blessed our family; and Hunter and Hayden, my two wonderful grandchildren who represent for me the reason to give my best in Bible study ministry which will one day encourage them to accept Christ and to serve the Lord with all their hearts.

Contents

Foreword

Having served at the Baptist Sunday School Board for 44 years, I confess to a protective spirit concerning its work and its future. This applies especially to the cause of the Sunday School—the Bible Teaching-Reaching phase of the Board's assignment.

When I learned that Harry Piland was retiring as director of this division, I was deeply concerned about who would succeed him. I wrote Harry that if the Board secured a person as effective as the one who followed me, I would be happy indeed! When I met with Bill Taylor and talked with him for the first time, I was well satisfied. Every contact with Bill since then has only deepened my appreciation for him and the strong commitment he has for the cause of Bible teaching and outreach in the churches and denomination.

After reading *21 Truths, Tradition, and Trends*, I know why I was so pleased with his selection to lead the division. He not only believes in the historical principles of Sunday School growth and ministry, but he has practiced them successfully in a number of our great churches. He brings with him to this new assignment convictions and experiences which admirably equip him for this significant leadership position for Southern Baptists. As you study this book Bill has prepared, you will find it both stimulating and reassuring that he is leading us into the 21st century.

—A. V. Washburn

When I received Bill Taylor's manuscript *21 Truths, Traditions, & Trends*, I glanced over the chapters and thought, *I must read that NOW!* I became so caught up with the book I could not lay it down until I had read every word. *21 Truths, Traditions, and Trends* is right for our times. As we approach the 21st century, pastors, ministers of education, and lay Sunday School leaders will find this book offers thoughtful and helpful insights for the reaching, teaching, and witnessing ministries of our churches. When everything nailed down seems to be coming loose in the world and in the church, it is most

vi

encouraging to read this significant book from a mature, wise, and proven leader like Bill Taylor.

This book is unique. It is easy to read, enjoyable, informative, and inspiring. Bill writes in a warm, personal style, and from extensive experience. He has been in the trenches. He has done the job. He has proven himself. He uses many pertinent and practical illustrations. The illustrations are from experience and right where we live.

His writing is straightforward, direct, clear, and easy to understand. Yet the content is meaty—even profound, especially the principles espoused. He carefully traces some of our SBC traditions and points out significant basic truths which we hold. He then carefully notes some significant trends that are of great importance in achieving the Great Commission as we approach the 21st century. He is unwilling to throw away past truths and principles but is eager to explore and consider emerging trends.

Taylor clearly defines Sunday School, points out its roots in Scripture, and thoughtfully and appreciatively views its historical perspective. He knows Sunday School, and he knows Sunday School history. Pioneers like Robert Raikes, E. Y. Mullins, James Frost, Arthur Flake, and Jasper Barnette are treated with respect, appreciation, and gratitude. Taylor shares his own personal pilgrimage with us. From his roots we learn of his intensity and caring passion for Sunday School, Bible study, and reaching people.

He rightly encourages churches and leaders of the 1990s to place a renewed emphasis on leadership training and teaching and reaching excellence. He holds that we have seen a decline of quality teaching and reaching and ministering, and he is right. Taylor's ministry, I predict, will be sharply focused on excellence in these areas. It is time for such an emphasis.

Further, Bill Taylor reminds us of the importance of teamwork, hard work, and thorough preparation in Sunday School work. Indeed there is no substitute. If these things do not happen, our mission will not be done. There is a tendency to cut corners in our fast-moving world. Bill reminds us there is a price for excellence.

He implores SBC churches to realize the significance and importance of the laity in the Sunday School movement. He recognizes—as did Flake, Mullins, Frost, Barnette, and other early leaders—that Sunday School is a lay movement and that the church can never achieve its objective without the full participation of the laity. Taylor reminds us that churches will never have enough paid staff to do the work they are called to do. Having been a staff member of proven experience, he knows the importance of a God-called staff but is sure that the work will never be done with staff alone.

Bill Taylor reveals his own great vision as he encourages churches and leaders to seek what God wants to do through us. His emphasis in chapter 9 on "seeing" is especially inspiring. Taylor reminds us that, if you cannot see it before you see it, you will never see it.

His chapter on innovation and tradition is a highlight. It should be read by every church leader and member. His insistence on a basic system is encouraging and on target.

Taylor believes in excellence in all areas and especially excellence in communication. He strongly encourages educational leaders to use the best communication tools of our day and to be an example for our people. He is a marvelous example and leader for us all in this area.

He sees the future as bright and promising. A positive believer who has one foot firmly planted in solid tradition and timeless truth, Taylor has the other foot planted in the significant emerging trends that are here and on the horizon.

As I completed the manuscript, I laid it down and concluded with a brief prayer, "Thank you, Lord, for bringing Bill Taylor to Southern Baptist churches and Sunday Schools."

Sunday School work is in good hands. He is the right man at the right time for the right job. He will lead us well. The best days for Sunday School work and reaching and teaching the multitudes is not behind us but before us. Amen and Amen!

—Harry Piland

Preface

"And God said, 'Let there be light,' and there was light" (Gen. 1:3, NIV).[1] This light of God has been the source to guide His people throughout the centuries since the time of creation.

As we look to the close of the 20th century and to the beginning of the 21st century, the light of God will continue to light our paths. In the Christian education realm, God has lighted the paths for persons like J. M. Frost, B. W. Spilman, Robert Raikes, J. N. Barnette, A. V. Washburn, Jim Neyland, and Harry Piland to lead Christians toward the 21st century of Bible teaching.

To go into the 21st century, God has called an outstanding Christian educator, Bill Taylor, to lead Christians to light a dark world with the knowledge of the Word of God. In this book, Taylor shares his personal philosophy of Christian education and his beliefs that Bible Teaching-Reaching Ministry is essential for God to provide light in a dark world.

This book, *21 Truths, Traditions, and Trends,* can propel the Sunday School into the 21st century. It will serve as a traditional-based challenge to ignite God's light in the hearts of pastors, staff, Sunday School leaders, and members. It shows that Sunday School is still relevant in God's plan for teaching and reaching. The book challenges Christian educators to build upon the past, focus on the present, and propel into the next century using God's light for a dark world.

The ideas and teachings in this book are based on the work of Christian educators of yesterday and the leaders of today. Taylor also boldly predicts trends for the next century of Bible Teaching-Reaching Ministry.

This book shows how the power of God has worked through Sunday School to light a dark world. Taylor's confidence in the ongoing desire for people to gether to study God's Word gives hope for future generations.

Most chapters include the use of three icons:

The candle identifies traditions of Christian education. These are views and practices that have been a foundation of Christian education from the past and continue to be valuable today and shall be tomorrow.

The torch will bring a focus of light on basic principles or truths of Christian education which have been a basis of Sunday School work for many years and will be a basis throughout the future until the Lord returns.

The third icon is the laser. As the laser beam is valuable for lights of medicine to lights of entertainment, so Christian education must identify with the needs of the 21st century. Methods, procedures, and resources of Christian education must rise to 21st-century challenges to lead God's light into the world of tomorrow. The laser will help us to identify these trends.

Sunday School is a powerful Christian education ministry. Bible Teaching-Reaching can change lives. Through Christian education the Spirit of God can light a dark world. May God use *21 Truths, Traditions, and Trends* to be a source of energetic knowledge to help your church light a dark world. "Let your light shine before men, that they may see your good deeds and praise your Father in Heaven" (Matt. 5:16, NIV).

—Garry W. Insko

[1]From the Holy Bible, *New International Version*, copyright © 1973, 1978, 1984 by International Bible Society. Subsequent quotations are marked NIV.

x

Chapter 1

A Word of Encouragement

"**I** am glad you have taken in hand that blessed work of setting up Sunday Schools in Chester. I wonder Satan has not yet sent out some able champion against them."

—John Wesley (1787)

This is a book of encouragement and hope. My desire is to remind the reader of the wonderful heritage we have as believers, and I want readers to consider the vast potential of the Sunday School movement for the 21st century.

During the latter part of the 19th century, the famous preacher and scholar Basil Manly lifted up the hearts of the leaders of his day by challenging them to embrace what he called "the great missionary to the future—the Sunday School."

The work of the Sunday School is far-reaching. No organization in the world has had greater influence on the Christian community than the Sunday School. Hundreds of thousands of people have come to Christ, and larger numbers have grown in the maturity of the Lord because of the power of what some have called "the church organized."

Sunday School was—and is—the great missionary to the future.

The Sunday School has long been on the front lines of recruitment of workers, and legions of leaders have matured under its tutelage. Those recruited church leaders have used the Sunday School as one of their major sources of communication about important events in the life and work of the congregation. When one considers how many assignments and tasks have been placed on this organization, the influence of this approach in ministry is staggering.

In a day when the Sunday School may not seem to have many champions, I want to be one who will say a good word about this God-blessed, God-led system of reaching, teaching, winning, and developing people for Christ.

Years ago the song "Happiness Is" was popular. Its carefree melody and words carried a message that happiness is different things to different people. The same meaning could be applied to Sunday School. Sunday School is different things to different people.

• To some people Sunday School is primarily for children.

• To the uninformed speaker Sunday School is elementary, shallow, or a great place to get a chuckle.

• To a few leaders Sunday School is outdated—a reminder of the way things were done in the past.

• To the church surveyor Sunday School is obsolete. A paradigm shift is required for the future.

• To some leaders Sunday School is a babysitter—a place to keep the children while meaningful activities are planned for adults.

• To other leaders Sunday School is the

12

church organized—the organization used by the church to direct the resources of ministry.

To those who value Sunday School, who've experienced its worth, Sunday School is many good things.

• Sunday School is a Bible seminary in its finest sense, where more people study the Word of God than through any other means in the world.

• Sunday School is the church's teaching-learning center, where millions of people have grown to maturity in Christ and have been taught to be leaders.

• Sunday School is an evangelism center, where countless masses have come to know Christ as personal Savior.

• Sunday School is the good Samaritan center of compassion, where meaningful care and personal attention are applied to the hurts of the world.

• Sunday School is an employment agency, where new believers and members find their first place of service in the body of Christ.

• Sunday School is the church-growth center, where more new classes and new churches are born than any other place in the world.

• Sunday School, with the Woman's Missionary Union and Baptist Men, is the world missions pipeline, from which resources, in both personnel and offerings, have been channeled to mission causes around the world.

• Sunday School is the strategic plan, combined with congregational worship, which has the potential to involve and direct the ministry and missionary activities of the body of Christ.

• Sunday School is the true north compass

Through Sunday School many have come to know Christ as personal Savior.

13

Sunday School enables churches to fulfill the Great Commission.

which has kept churches around the world forever focused on their target of evangelism and Bible study, thus fulfilling the directives of the Great Commission.

• Sunday School is still the "great missionary to the future," poised to reenergize its strengths and to reinvent itself to be the most powerful force of the 21st century.

The truths, traditions, and trends, which will be shared in the remainder of this book, seek to examine the history of the Sunday School movement, make a correct analysis of its current usage and corresponding effectiveness, and promote the values to its continued employment in the forthcoming millennium.

A nine-year-old girl darted by me one Sunday, and I told her that I liked her new hair style. She stopped in her tracks, looked me in the eyes, extended her hand toward me, and exclaimed, "Thank you for that word of encouragement."

I want to give you a word of encouragement as we look at truths, traditions, and trends of the Sunday School.

Personal Learning Activities

1. What does "Sunday School is the great missionary to the future" mean?

2. In your own words, complete the sentence, Sunday School is. . . .

14

Chapter 2

A Journey from Confusion to Certainty

"**S**end me anywhere. . . only go with me. Lay on me any burden. . . only sustain me. Sever any cord save the tie that binds me to thy service."

—David Livingstone (1838)

My basic training was in music, and I served as a minister of music for about 13 years. In 1973, I made a career change to the ministry of education. Even though I had completed a master of religious education degree, most of the actions I initiated during my first months in this new role were modeled after what I had seen practiced in education ministries of the local church. I calendared traditional high-attendance days and was constantly on the lookout for a new theme or promotional idea. Weekly searches of various church bulletins which came through the church office yielded ideas, which shortly appeared in the publications of my church.

After going through this process for almost a year, I grew weary of this common practice of "hype." I remember looking into the

Sunday School is "the church organized."

eyes of the members and leaders and seeing almost an emptiness and a lack of support for this approach to ministry. My prayer in those days was, "Lord, if you allow me the privilege of serving another 30 years, I don't think I can continue using this approach." Basically, I didn't enjoy what I was encouraging the members to do. I literally did not know where to turn for help.

Not long after that I received a telephone call from Nolan Johnston, the education minister for the New Orleans Association. He told me that the Baptist Sunday School Board was working with Louisiana Baptists, sponsoring a state training conference at First Baptist Church of Bossier City, in January 1973. He thought I would profit from attending this meeting. Soon after his call, I received a brochure with the details of the meeting.

I asked my Sunday School director, Jim Simmons, to accompany my wife, Rose, and me to this training seminar. I left New Orleans not realizing what drastic changes God would be making in my life during the next three days.

Little did I realize that I would be introduced to two experts in building Bible study ministries. One would become almost like a father to me, and the other I would know only through the printed page and the results of his ministry.

I walked into that meeting and listened to a Southern Baptist educator use a term I had never heard before. He talked about "the church organized." Soon it was apparent that the speaker was referring to the Sunday School.

He continued to challenge the partic-

16

ipants with the following statements:

• "If you want to reach hundreds of people for Christ, build the 'church organized.'"

• "If you want to raise millions of dollars for world missions, reinforce the work of the Bible study units."

• "If you want to be able to build facilities which house Bible study classes, direct your energies toward strengthening the small-group ministry."

• "If you desire to be instrumental in enlisting and equipping men and women to be effective in ministry, direct your attention to the ministry of the Sunday School."

• "If you wish to make a great impact for your Lord in the days ahead, take steps to ensure that the Sunday School organization not only grows but also flourishes."

Jim Neyland was that educator, and he spoke with great authority because he was one of the leading practitioners in the emerging field of church growth. At that time he was serving as minister of education at Dauphin Way Baptist Church in Mobile, Alabama.

Jim was saved in 1947 at First Baptist Church, Lake Charles, Louisiana, at the age of 24. His new bride, Ruby, was instrumental in leading him to accept Christ.

His first experience in Sunday School work was being enrolled in a men's Bible study class. The roll listed 24 men, but only 4 were present the first time he attended. Jim's immediate response to the teacher was, "Where are the other 20 members, and how can we reach them for Bible study?" This love for people typified his 40 years of service.

Through the organization called Sunday School churches have reached people for Christ, raised money for missions, built facilities, equipped men and women for ministry, and greatly impacted the world.

17

The Sunday School was and is a great way to grow a church.

Jim was asked to be a group captain and finally the class president. He was told that if he followed the steps in a pamphlet given to him by the teacher he would be able to do his job well. That resource was published by the Sunday School Board.

Jim was so successful at the class level that he was asked to be the superintendent of the Sunday School at First Baptist Church. Soon a new pastor, Paul Roberts, was called to the church. Because of Jim's inexperience and young age, he offered his resignation to the new pastor, not wanting to hinder any work the new pastor might want to attempt.

Robert's response to Jim was, "Would you like to become the most effective Sunday School superintendent in the Southern Baptist Convention?"

Jim was challenged by the proposition and encouraged that the new pastor could see leadership potential in his life. When Jim responded, "Yes!" Roberts told him to "hang on to your hat! We are going to burn up the woods."

The mentoring process between these two godly men led the way for First Baptist Church of Lake Charles to triple in all phases of its ministry during the next few years. The response of the people was so great that it soon became obvious that God was leading this young businessman into the education ministry. This call led to further preparation for service at Southwestern Baptist Theological Seminary in Fort Worth, Texas.

Putting into practice the basic principles of Sunday School expansion taught by his pastor and religious education professors, Jim

18

led every church he served to flourish in numerical and spiritual growth. First Baptist Church, Hurst, Texas, his seminary church; Columbus Avenue Baptist Church, Waco, Texas; and First Baptist Church, West Monroe, Louisiana, grew under his leadership in the area of Christian education.

Jim became recognized as one of the leading Sunday School consultants in America. Then Jaroy Weber asked Jim to join him in reestablishing a declining church in Alabama, the historic Dauphin Way Baptist Church. Soon it became one of the first megachurches in America, exceeding three thousand people in Bible study in the early 70s, which was rare at the time.

From that background of being a proven leader in Sunday School expansion, Jim Neyland challenged the conferees in Louisiana to build the "church organized."

He picked up an old Church Study Course book, produced by the Sunday School Board, and spoke of the man who had written this book. That was the first time I remember hearing the name of this person, a person who was to become my model of ministry in the days ahead. The name of the book was *A Church Using Its Sunday School* by J. N. Barnette.[1]

I had heard the term "a million more in '54," but I did not connect J. N. Barnette to it. Barnette served as an associate of Arthur Flake from 1927 to 1943. From 1943 to 1957 he was secretary of the Sunday School Department (a position similar to the post I now command as director of the Bible Teaching-Reaching Division).[2]

"A million more in '54" enrolled 597,000 new people in Sunday School in one year. This number has not been surpassed in any year since that time.

19

The Sunday School is the mainstay organization in the overall ministry of the church.

Barnette led Southern Baptists to attempt to have a net gain in enrollment of one million people in one year. The final number was 597,000 new people in Bible study enrollment, a number never even closely matched during the 42 years since the "million more in '54" campaign.

I almost hesitate to admit that I had that book in my library and had never opened its pages. The librarian at Field Street Baptist Church in Cleburne, Texas—my seminary church—had given me copies of older study course books which she was discarding; and I had placed them on my shelves, never realizing how valuable their teachings were and are even today. J. N. Barnette is so important to discussions of Bible study ministry that I have included a later chapter which deals with the influence of his life and the principles of church growth which he advocated.

I doubt that Jim Neyland realized, when he completed his assignment in Bossier City, that he had been used of the Lord to redirect the life of a young man who decided to see if the teachings of that Sunday School seminar would really work. But on that Saturday night, when I rode in the car with my wife, Rose, and Jim Simmons, on our return to Memorial Baptist Church in Metarie, Louisiana, our lively discussion centered around what we had learned in those brief days of training. Silently, I thought, I can't wait to get back to the "city which care forgot" to see if those principles will work.

Since that strategic meeting, I have discovered that Jim Neyland was right about that

20

which he was sharing. I have experienced the following:

• The basic principles of organizational expansion do work as exhibited in the hundreds of growing churches.

• Sunday School is an effective way to reach multitudes of people in Bible study.

• Many people have accepted Christ as their personal Savior through the Sunday School.

• Resources have been provided to take care of the needs of missions, facilities, and whatever was needed to strengthen the Lord's work in a community.

• Bible study leaders grow in their walk with God as they serve through the Sunday School.

• God has used the "church organized" to make a lasting impact throughout the world.

It has now been 23 years since that significant event occurred in my life. I can testify that those statements were not only true, but they also held more promise for my own life and the lives of the people which I have encountered since those days of training in North Louisiana.

As a part of his own personal stewardship, Jim Neyland has always given two weeks of his time each year to the Sunday School Board to teach Bible study organization principles to people across America. One of those assignments was in Bossier City. He made a difference, even when he did not know that the future director of the Bible Teaching-Reaching Division was sitting at his feet, eagerly learning from his experience and wisdom.

Today, as you read this book, if you, too, have the privilege of sharing, give your best. Continue to challenge the young men and

Sunday School has provided on-the-job training for thousands of church leaders.

21

Reaching and teaching go hand in hand.

women of our churches to build and strengthen the Bible study organizations. Because of the rapid changes of the last 10 years in every realm of life, there are probably more young educators who are confused about what is really significant in the execution of their responsibilities. There is a crying need for more dedicated leaders such as Jim Neyland to encourage young potential leaders, just as Paul Roberts encouraged him. Who knows who could be the J. N. Barnette of the next millennium. The "church organized" is just as effective today as it was 22 years ago, and it still holds the promise of being effective into the 21st century.

Personal Learning Activities

1. Describe the differences between programs by "hype" and ministry through the "church organized."

2. Jim Neyland and J. N. Barnette are two heroes of Sunday School work. Who are your personal heroes or mentors? If possible, call or write to express your appreciation. Thank God for their ministry and for their impact on your ministry and the growth of God's kingdom.

[1]J. N. Barnette, *A Church Using Its Sunday School* (Nashville: The Sunday School Board of the Southern Baptist Convention, 1937).
[2]*Encyclopedia of Southern Baptists*, III, 1609.

22

Chapter 3
The Sunday School Movement —a Historical Perspective

"From God's own hand, Sunday School is a gift from heaven."

—W. A. Criswell (1995)[1]

Three events, typical of the challenges faced in the propagation of Bible studies, relied solely on the Great Commission for their mission and direction:

1. When the first Sunday School met in Richmond, Virginia, in what was to become the First Baptist Church, the pastor, "Father Courtney," "considered the Sunday School a desecration of the Lord's Day and heartily disapproved, calling it a secular institution. Those leading the Sunday School soon withdrew their membership and began another church."[2]

2. In 1899, B. W. Spilman was met at the county line in Princeton, North Carolina, with a note which stated, "Be it resolved,

23

Sunday School advocates have often faced difficulties and opposition.

that no man advocating Sunday schools, Bible societies, or any other institutions of the day, shall be allowed to travel through our borders."[3] He went on to speak there, however, and even used the resolution as part of his address.

3. When J. M. Frost brought forth the resolution which would establish the Sunday School Board at the 1891 meeting of the Southern Baptist Convention, he was forced to concede to another leader about restrictions on this new work. He had to be pulled through a window in order to get to the platform to present the proposal.[4]

Ever since the first Sunday School was introduced, champions of this great cause have faced an uphill battle. They have often been thrown out, kept out, and forced to enter through side entrances. Many leaders today with the spirit of "Father Courtney" would associate themselves from the Sunday School movement. But understanding the difficulties and battles faced by Sunday School leaders of the past helps church leaders today understand how obvious the hand of God has been on the life and work of the Sunday School movement.

To understand fully the Sunday School movement, one needs to examine what the Bible says concerning instructions and opportunities for learning. Even though the actual Sunday School is only about 215 years old, there are accounts in the Bible of various schools and times of learning.

Old Testament

Genesis 14:14 reveals that Abraham had 318 trained men, born in his household.

24

"*Trained*" or "instructed" conveys the idea of a school or a period of instruction.

"The Lord was with Jehoshaphat because he walked in the first ways of his father David" (2 Chron. 17:3). Jehoshaphat also sent priests and Levites through the country who "taught in Judah, and had the book of the law of the Lord with them, and went about throughout all the cities of Judah and taught the people" (2 Chron. 17:9). These were traveling Bible schools, taught by the finest teachers in the land.

One of the best descriptions of a Sunday School is found in Nehemiah 8. It includes place, organization, administrator, teachers, devotional materials, and classwork. Verse 8 provides the best description of teaching to be found: "So they read in the book of the law of God distinctly, and gave the sense, and caused them to understand the reading." They literally "caused them to understand." Teaching is causing another to understand.

The heritage of the Sunday School is rich and colorful.

Jewish History

Consider these stories from history:
• Josephus, the famous Jewish historian, claimed that from the time of Moses it was the custom of the Jews to assemble every Sabbath, not only to hear the law read but also to learn it accurately.[5]

• Philo, antedating Josephus about 75 years, called synagogues, "houses of instruction," or as we would say "school buildings."[6]

• Jewish schools for Bible study were regarded as the life of the nation. "If you would

25

destroy the Jews, you must destroy the schools," was a maxim.

New Testament

Jewish tradition and history establish the value of biblical teaching/learning.

Jesus is our ultimate example:
- He considered Himself a teacher.
- His friends, foes, and followers considered Jesus a teacher.
- He taught masterfully, as no one ever before or afterwards.
- He commissioned His followers to teach.

The New Testament is filled with examples of Jesus teaching:
- Jesus, "being subject to his parents," would have attended established schools. "They found him in the temple courts, sitting among the teachers, listening to them and asking them questions" (Luke 2:46, NIV).[7]
- Matthew wrote, "Jesus went throughout Galilee teaching in their synagogues" (Matt. 4:23, NIV).
- The Great Commission is recorded in the phraseology of instruction: "Go teach," make disciples or learners, "train" (see Matt. 28:19-20).

Teaching in the New Testament extends beyond Jesus' personal ministry and the Gospels. The Book of Acts, for example, records that the apostles "ceased not to teach and preach Jesus" (Acts 5:42).

Paul also was a teacher. Consider these facts about Paul:
- He was educationally advantaged.
- He had a superior education.
- He was perceived as a teacher.
- His teaching was effective.

26

- He taught in synagogues.
- He taught whenever and wherever he could.
- He used a variety of methods.
- He admonished pastors to teach.
- He taught faithfully during his entire ministry.
- He taught with others. Paul and Barnabas continued in Antioch, "teaching and preaching the word of the Lord" (Acts 15:35).

Church History

Philip Schaff, in his *History of the Christian Church*, pointed out that after the days of the apostles no names of great missionaries are known or recorded until the opening of the Middle Ages. We know of no missionary societies, missionary institutions, or organized efforts during that period. Yet in less than three hundred years after John's death, the whole population of the Roman Empire, which then represented the civilized world, was nominally Christian.

The great teachers of the early centuries, such as Clement, at the head of the Alexandrian School; Origen, and Augustine attribute their success to catechetical teaching. Celsus, the powerful enemy of Christianity, accused Christians of advancing their cause by getting hold of the children in their schools. Origen admitted the charge but showed how the children were improved and benefited by the teaching.

St. Francis Xavier said, "Give me the children until they are seven years old, and anyone may have them after that."

The Bible provides the model for teaching God's Word.

27

Leaders of the Sunday School movement have always been visionary in scope and practice.

Martin Luther stated, "For the church's sake, Christian schools must be established and maintained."

With this dramatic backdrop of support for the teaching of God's Word, the Sunday School movement was born. Convinced that they were being led by the Spirit of God, men and women stepped forward, accepted the challenge, and readied themselves to make any sacrifice necessary to ensure that this grand opportunity would not be missed.

First Sunday School

Robert Raikes

Church historians do not agree about when the first Sunday School was established, but no one questions the contribution made by a young Englishman named Robert Raikes. His work among prisoners convinced him that religious education would help keep young people out of jail. Because so many children worked in factories every day except Sunday, he formed a school in 1780 that met on Sundays in the homes of lay teachers.

His first efforts were met with criticism on all fronts, especially from the clergy who seemed to be threatened by this new work. He and his schools were dubbed "Bobby Wildgoose and his ragged regiment." Undaunted, Raikes moved swiftly, establishing what must have seemed extreme measures to these "ragged regiments," when he put forth the basic requirements for participation—clean hands and faces and combed hair.[8]

28

Within four years of Raikes' first school in Gloucester, more than 250,000 children were enrolled in Bible study. By the time of his death in 1811, the weekly Sunday School attendance had grown to more than four hundred thousand.

John Wesley

John Wesley, the famous Methodist evangelist, was one of the first to embrace the Sunday School movement. His acknowledgement of its value is evident in the following statement: "I verily think these Sunday Schools are the noblest institutions which have been seen in Europe for some centuries, and will increase more and more."[9]

On another occasion, Wesley remarked, "The Sunday School is one of the noblest specimens of charity which has been set on foot in England since the days of William the Conqueror. . . . It will be one of the great means of reviving religious thought throughout the nation."[10]

The Sunday School idea, practically applied, has had great influence in national reforms and national prosperity. In the days of Robert Raikes, Lord Mahon pointed to the Sunday School as the beginning of a new era in the national life of England.

John Richard Green, the English historian, speaking of the dark days following the American Revolution, just after the beginning of Raikes' work, said: "It was then that the moral, the philanthropic, the religious ideas which have molded English society into its present

Jesus is our ultimate example. His teaching ministry continues to set the standard for teachers today.

29

The first national gathering of Sunday School leaders was held in 1832 for the purpose of training, establishing a pattern of equipping leaders.

shape, first broke the spiritual torpor of the eighteenth century."

The movement spread rapidly in England and Wales and was soon introduced in the United States.

First Sunday Schools in America

William Elliott is credited with starting the first Sunday School in the New World. In 1785, he set up a dual Bible study in his home, providing one hour of instruction for white students followed by another hour of teaching for black students. Sixteen years later, in 1801, the Sunday school was transferred to the Burton-Oak Grove Methodist Church, Brandfords Neck, Virginia.[11]

The second Sunday School was created one year after the first, in 1786, by Francis Asbury, in the home of Thomas Crenshaw of Hanover County, Virginia. Its purpose was to provide Bible instruction for the slaves on the plantation.[12]

First National Convention

The news about this new way of sharing Bible truths and allowing people of all stations the privilege of studying the Word of God spread rapidly across America. Within 31 years, after the first Sunday School moved onto church property, the first national gathering of Sunday School leaders was conducted in 1832 in Philadelphia.[13] The Honorable Theodore Frelinghuysen presided. Some of the topics offered at this first training session were:

30

• Infant Sunday School Organizations
• Qualifying Scholars to Become Teachers
• Propriety of Having More Than One Session a Day (Most Sunday School leaders think that dual Sunday Schools are a recent invention. The leaders of the Sunday School movement have always been visionary in scope and practice.)

First Adult Department

Perhaps because of its origins in England, when Robert Raikes initiated Bible study and helps for the ragamuffins of the streets of Gloucester, often the Sunday School has been viewed as an organization for children. More than 119 years passed before the first department specifically designed for adults was begun. It was started in the Calvary Baptist Church of Washington, D. C., in 1899. W. A. Duncan noted the importance of this event, "There has been no thought or plan so important and so far reaching in its possibilities since the first Sunday School was organized."

By 1909, adult work was beginning to become a part of more Southern Baptist churches. This was seen most clearly in the advent of the Baraca-Philathea classes for men and women.[14]

Sunday School Pioneers

The pages of history have no greater heroes than those who took up the cause of organized Bible study for the people of America. Known as Sunday School missionaries, these

From the time of its beginning through the present day, the Sunday School movement has experienced growth.

31

Stephen Paxson was limited in the eyes of the world but not in God's eyes. He played a significant role in spreading the work of the Sunday School.

giants of the faith blazed trails of conquest, not unlike what Lewis and Clark or Daniel Boone did for American society.

Stephen Paxson

One of those early Sunday school missionaries is Stephen Paxson. He is an example of a life considered of little value by the standards of the world and yet one that moved from despair to triumph. An unnamed Bible teacher reached out to Stephen and touched him in the spirit of a Robert Raikes, who loved the disadvantaged children of the streets of England.

Stephen was born crippled and had such a severe case of stuttering that when he was a child his peers called him "Stuttering Steve." His learning skills were so limited that he was denied the privilege of education, even in the primitive schools of his day. He actually learned to read by spelling out the letters on signboards. Stephen was self-educated without the assistance of an instructor.

God moved in his heart, and Stephen dedicated his life to sharing the message of Jesus and fostering new Sunday Schools across America. Undaunted by bad weather, he exclaimed, "A Sunday School born in a snowstorm will never be scared by a white frost."[15]

A major part of my assignment at the Sunday School Board is giving leadership in developing field services and resources for churches, associations, and state conventions. Several times a year my calendar fills with speaking engagements which cause me to be away from my family. I also work with a number of consultants who travel frequently. From time to

32

time, this hectic schedule causes me to express concern about how many hours I am working or that I am being denied time with my family.

Stephen Paxson would have loved to work as a Sunday School missionary today. His lifestyle in the 1800s put him on the road for several months at a time. He did not know the benefits of air travel we have today; rather he traveled over a hundred thousand miles by horseback, starting new Sunday Schools.

He rode one horse, named Robert Raikes, for more than 25 years. It was said that the horse Robert Raikes was so trained he would never pass a child on the road. The horse knew from Paxson's habitual lifestyle that the missionary would stop to invite that child to Sunday School.

Paxson organized 1,314 new Sunday Schools, enrolling more than 83 thousand members in Bible study. He also encouraged the ongoing work of another 1,747 schools. During one intensive period he organized 47 new Sunday Schools in 40 days. Is it any wonder that Sunday Schools flourished over the various states he visited?

The crown of his dedicated life came in New York City when "his aristocratic auditors were so deeply interested that they wept and smiled alternatively, never heeding mistakes in grammar or rhetorical discrepancies."[16] This self-educated, "Stuttering Steve" was used of God to leave a legacy of hope.

**B. W. Spilman—
the Sunday School Man**
One cannot understand the quality of disciple that B. W. Spilman was without an

More than a hundred years separated the beginning of the Sunday School movement and offering Sunday School classes for adults.

33

B. W. Spilman offered the first teacher training correspondence courses for Sunday School workers, the first of many innovations in leadership training.

insight into the day-to-day practices of this unique man of God. To say that Bernard W. Spilman was driven by his love for Christ and his faithfulness to sharing the gospel barely addresses the subject.

While preaching at the Raleigh Tabernacle Church, Spilman fainted in the pulpit. After an extended illness, his physician, W. I. Royster, sounded an ominous note when he warned the headstrong preacher, "It is written across the tablet of your heart that if you take the field again, you will certainly be dead in less than ninety days."[17] When the afternoon train pulled out of the station, B. W. Spilman was on it, facing the threat of death rather than laying down the assignment he loved so much.

In 1896, Spilman sent a call to the churches of North Carolina, asking for information regarding their ministries. He discovered that four hundred churches had no Sunday School and only six Sunday Schools were well organized and adequately equipped. He found no interest in missions, and most of the churches did virtually nothing to spread the good news. From his initial research came forth the first Sunday School Institute, a school of methods and a means of interesting people in Bible study organization.

One of his first experiments was teacher training courses offered by correspondence. R. L. Moore of Mars Hills, a lawyer, was the first enrollee. To get a grasp of how innovative this approach was at the time, one has to see it in comparison to teleconferencing possibilities today.

Often when Spilman traveled across

34

the state of North Carolina, he carried a tent with him in which five or six people could sleep. During many of his summer meetings, he slept in the tent so others could sleep in homes of residents who opened their doors to those leading the Sunday School meetings. He also carried a paper blanket made of the kind of paper on which money is printed. He found that it offered additional warmth in many conditions.[18]

In 1892, the Board appropriated $3,000 of its slim means to the different state organizations for Sunday School and missionary work. Then in 1901, J. M. Frost invited B. W. Spilman to be the first field secretary for the Sunday School Board. Spilman was noted as having offices in three places: a meager location at the Board, railroad stations, and the wayside.

The guidelines for Spilman's assignments were as follows:

1. Work toward the improvement of Sunday Schools in Southern states.

2. Work in cooperation with the person in charge of Sunday School work in each state.

3. Accept no compensation except room and meals.

4. Go only at the invitation of people of that state.

5. Give none of his time to selling Sunday School literature. Frost viewed field work as a gift of the Baptist Sunday School Board to Baptist churches.[19]

The spirit and exemplary lives of these Sunday School pioneers was typical of many who made similar sacrifices. Further examination brings to mind others such as P. E.

Serving as a Sunday School missionary has never been easy, but it's always rewarding.

35

The annals of Sunday School ministry are filled with the names of those who practiced excellence and far-sightedness in making sure that whatever was needed was provided.

Burroughs, Landrum Leavell, Arthur Flake, and J. N. Barnette. Recent advocates such as A. V. Washburn, Harry Piland, and Elsie Rives will one day be considered for the Sunday School "Hall of Fame."

We pay homage to the Robert Raikes, Stephen Paxsons, and the B. W. Spilmans; but the annals of Sunday School ministry are filled with the names of those who practiced excellence and far-sightedness in making sure that whatever was needed was provided. These unnamed heroes are part of the historical perspective which has been blessed by God in its creation and execution and has, in turn, been a blessing to the hundreds of thousands of people who have matured in the work of the Lord as a result of their participation in the Sunday School movement.

It is not your choice to be among those whose names are recognized as stellar leaders among Christian leaders or to be one of the countless faithful servants who are recognized only by the Lord. Your choice is to be obedient.

You may never be a target of ridicule as Stephen Paxson was, and you may never board a train with an ominous prediction of your death as B. W. Spilman did, but you can make an acceptable sacrifice in ministry. Count yourself blessed to be included in such a mighty army of disciples.

Personal Learning Activities
1. Did early Sunday Schools find church leaders eagerly welcoming them as an innovative tool to reach children for Christ, or did they

36

oppose this movement? Explain.

2. Compare and contrast Jesus and Paul as teachers.

3. Describe the contribution to the Sunday School movement of Robert Raikes, John Wesley, William Elliott, Stephen Paxson, or B. W. Spilman.

[1] W. A. Criswell, Alabama Sunday School Convention, Hunter St. Baptist Church, 1995.

[2] Belle Gayle Ellyson, *The History of the Second Baptist Church, Richmond, Virginia, 1820–1970* (Richmond: Second Baptist Church, 1981), 4.

[3] C. Sylvester Green, *B. W. Spilman: The Sunday School Man* (Nashville: Broadman Press, 1986), 45.

[4] J. M. Frost, *The Sunday School Board of the Southern Baptist Convention: Its History and Work* (Nashville: Sunday School Board of the Southern Baptist Convention, 1914), 20.

[5] Clarence H. Benson, *The Sunday School in Action* (Chicago: The Bible Institute Colportage Association, 1932), 13.

[6] Ibid.

[7] From the Holy Bible, *New International Version*, copyright © 1973, 1978, 1984 by International Bible Society. Subsequent quotations are followed by NIV.

[8] Benson, 15-16.

[9] Ibid., 16-17.

[10] Ibid.

[11] Frank Glenn Lankard, *A History of the American Sunday School Curriculum* (New York: Abingdon, 1927), 59.

[12] Ibid.

[13] Benson, 20.

[14] Louis B. Hanks, *Vision, Variety, and Vitality: Teaching Today's Adult Generations* (Nashville: Convention Press, 1996), 53.

[15] Edwin Wilbur Rice, *The Sunday School Movement and the American Sunday-School Union 1780-1927* (Philadelphia: The Union Press, 1917), 272.

[16] Ibid., 273.

[17] Green, 39.

[18] Ibid., 45-46.

[19] Ibid., 59-61.

Spilman later became the first Sunday School consultant, instructed by J. M. Frost to train workers as a gift to the churches, thus beginning a work that continues today.

Chapter 4

Flake and Barnette—Sunday School's Dynamic Duo

"It is not the critic who counts, not the man who points out how the strong man stumbles or where the doer of deeds could have done them better. The credit belongs to the man who is actually in the arena, whose face is marred by dust and sweat and blood, who strives valiantly, who errs and comes short again and again because there is no effort without error and shortcomings, who knows the great devotion, who spends himself in a worthy cause."

—**Theodore Roosevelt**

Only about half of Southern Baptist churches had Sunday Schools in 1900. Twenty-six years later, Sunday Schools were found in 84 percent of churches cooperating with the Southern Baptist Convention.

39

"No price is too great to pay; no sacrifice too great to make; no trial too heavy to endure, if we may attain the highest aim of life, the supreme blessing of mankind through the Gospel of Jesus Christ."
—Constance M. Parker

What brought about such a dramatic increase in such a brief period? Was it because the concept of using small-group Bible study finally found favorable roots? Was the growth of the movement fostered by the same phenomena as in other areas of society?

I think the answer is obvious. It was leadership, leadership, leadership.

The Sunday School Board, led by visionary founder J. M. Frost, moved aggressively into the promotion of Bible study units throughout the country. In 1901, he appointed B. W. Spilman to serve as a "field worker."

The leaders of the Sunday School Board, following Frost's example, made another crucial decision by enlisting Arthur Flake to serve as the first leader of the Sunday School Department.

Flake initiated a systematic approach in Bible study ministry—discover prospects, organize to reach people, enlist and train workers, provide space, and visit and enlist the prospects. Flake's system provided Baptists with a methodology that fit the times.[1]

The Board's next significant decision was to ask a farmer to join Arthur Flake in further developing this church-centered partnership between the churches and the Sunday School Board. Jasper N. Barnette was that farmer. He would ultimately be used to reach more people for systematic Bible study than anyone before or after his period of leadership.

One would be hard pressed to find two individuals who have had as much influence on modern-day Bible study ministry as Arthur Flake and J. N. Barnette. They were col-

40

leagues at the Sunday School Board, beginning in the 1920s. Both of them served at one time as secretary of the Sunday School Department. Both were laymen.

Today their legacy lives on—one because he created the "science of Sunday School growth," commonly referred to as the "Flake Formula for Growth," and the other because of his compassion for people and his phenomenal record of reaching people, as typified by the grandiose "Million More in '54" campaign.

Before either of these men were called to serve Southern Baptists, they were effective in their own local ministries. They were successful practitioners. They did not talk about building Sunday Schools; they built Sunday Schools. They had credibility as local-church practitioners before they began to work with churches on a national level.

Arthur Flake

Arthur Flake was a successful businessman. Once a traveling salesman, he entered the department store business in Winona, Mississippi, in 1894. All of this experience, even before he became a Christian, was in the providence of God, training him and developing in him abilities which were to be blessed and used of God later in the achievement of wonderful things for the kingdom.

Arthur Flake was Sunday School superintendent at Winona Baptist Church, Winona, Mississippi. Using his business acumen, he studied the Sunday School, recognized

Flake's Formula— discover prospects, organize to reach people, enlist and train workers, provide space, visit and enlist the prospects.

41

Work is a common ingredient in successful Sunday Schools in all generations.

its needs, and developed the practical methods that have so completely revolutionized Sunday School work. He built his own Sunday School and did it so sanely and so successfully that its work commanded attention throughout Mississippi.

Others wanted to hear what was working in Flake's Sunday School. Why? Because it was working; it was making a difference. I submit to you that if Arthur Flake had not built a strong Bible teaching ministry in Winona, Mississippi, we would never have heard his name outside that rural community.

One aspect of Flake's ministry which is not often noted is his dedication to discipleship. In 1895, he organized and became president of the Baptist Young People's Union in the Winona Baptist Church. He knew that Bible study was the foundation and beginning point, but believers had to move to a deeper level of commitment.

I like this aspect of Flake's life and ministry. As a minister of education, I always fostered discipleship. Bible study and discipleship go hand in hand in building a great church. That's one reason I value my friendship and opportunity to work with Roy Edgemon as he leads the work of discipleship and family ministry at the Sunday School Board. Together we can help churches develop a wholistic approach to ministry.

Flake's crowning work came in 1920 when I. J. Van Ness appointed him to establish and develop the work of Sunday School administration. There were no guideposts, no textbooks in the field, no literature or plans to fol-

42

low. There was need for vision to see, wisdom to think and plan, courage to dare, and energy to carry through.

Ever on the practical side, telling how improvement could be brought about, Flake exemplified the educator on mission. Yet his methods are so imbedded in scriptural truths and are built so clearly to meet human needs that his presentation of them was inspiration personified.

His contributions included these:

• He made the Standard of Excellence a guide for the future.

• He perfected the Six-Point Record System, building value into this phase of ministry.

• He championed the cause of weekly officers and teachers meetings, saying, "No Sunday school, anywhere, can do its best work without it."

• He planted his "5 Steps in Building a School" into the psyche of Southern Baptists.

• He insisted on using the association to foster Bible study in the churches.

• He created Sunday School enlargement campaigns.

But perhaps his most famous challenge is one which needs an audience today. Nothing can take the place of the one ingredient crucial to success—work. Arthur Flake was known for his conviction that work is the essential element to build a Sunday School—work, work, work. It was not easy to build a Bible study class in 1920. It is not easy today. It certainly will be difficult in the 21st century, but one thing is sure: It will take work.

God uses "plain" people—laypersons—like Arthur Flake and J. N. Barnette—to do His work.

43

J. N. Barnette

Dedicated leaders—such as J. N. Barnette—command the loyalty of all Sunday School workers who follow them.

What personal traits or feats cause us to remember J. N. Barnette? A recent conversation with Barnette's son-in-law, Roupen M. Gulbenk, sheds light on these factors.

During the spring of 1995, Barnette's family made a gift to the Sunday School Board of a portrait of this great Bible study leader. The portrait had hung in the parlor of the Gulbenk home for many years; but, because of the contribution which the Board had made to their family, the family felt that this painting should be a part of the history of the Sunday School Board. Jimmy Draper invited me to receive the painting from the Gulbenk family on behalf of the Bible Teaching-Reaching Division.

During and after the presentation in the weekly chapel service, Gulbenk told anecdotes related to Barnette's life and exactly what kind of person he was. According to Gulbenk, J. N. Barnette was a quiet, somber personality. A modest, humble, and unassuming gentleman, he was always interested in the individual.

He possessed abundant energy. He never seemed to tire. He remembered people. He was attentive to details. He sought consensus and spent much time making sure that everyone was in the loop regarding whatever issue was discussed.

Barnette started his adult life as a schoolteacher and farmer. At age 34, his reputation in Sunday School work led to a call from North Carolina Baptists to serve as an associate in the state convention Sunday School Department. Six years later he moved to the

44

Sunday School Board to lead in southwide, rural and associational Sunday School development.

Barnette appeared to dedicate himself wholly to Jesus Christ. Nothing could dim his vision that evangelism is basic in kingdom growth and that Bible study in Sunday School is the best way to teach people about their responsibility to reach people and motivate them to witness.

A. V. Washburn said that Barnette believed the program and ministry were worth whatever it cost him. "He didn't have a conviction; the conviction had him."

It was this dedication that commanded the loyalty of all Sunday School leaders. He never expected an associate to do more than he did. He was a personally involved leader, and his involvement was contagious. Those around him felt they were in the most important work in the world. There was no thought of defeat. His infectious spirit spread, and Southern Baptists sensed the urgency and importance of Sunday School at a time when some larger denominations were referring to Sunday School procedures as childish.

Barnette always had great confidence in "plain people." He believed that "plain people" could be enlisted, trained, and developed to do great tasks for God. This conviction caused him to inspire great numbers of people to invest their talents in the work of Christ. His confidence in them caused them to believe in themselves. His ability to motivate and inspire individuals to achieve goals which they felt were unattainable proved to be one of his greatest leadership contributions.

Ordinary people can be enlisted, trained, and developed to do great tasks for God.

45

Committed workers will never know how many people they will influence through their ministry.

Example to His Consultants

Travel.—Barnette and W. P. Phillips had a contest in their annual drive to the summer conference center at Ridgecrest as to who could use the least amount of gasoline on the trip from Nashville. They would coast down the hills to conserve fuel, thereby freeing up funds which could be used in other areas of work at the Sunday School Board.

Work.—After a full day of teaching in the educational classes at Ridgecrest and the completion of the worship service in Spilman Auditorium, Barnette would go to the dining hall and mop the floors, helping to get ready for the next day.

Bob Edd Shotwell, retired minister of education, Hyde Park Baptist Church, Austin, Texas, and Harry Piland spoke to me at the 1995 Sunday School training weeks at Glorieta about J. N. Barnette's ministry. Bob Edd and Harry were in their 20s during the 1950s. When they attended Glorieta in those days, they would try to position their chairs as near as possible to the faculty table in the dining hall. J. N. Barnette, A. V. Washburn, Herman King, and E. A. Herron sat together each day, discussing Bible study strategies.

As I listened to Bob Edd and Harry, who have been used so mightily in our generation, speak of their loyalty to these leaders of the past, I wondered if Barnette ever knew how many people his example of leadership would influence at a later date through the ministries of these two young men who heard him speak.

Henry Love, retired minister of education, summed up the contributions of J. N.

46

Barnette when he wrote: "The Sunday School in our modern churches is not an 'hour.' It is a power! It is not an isolated project; it is a program of work. Barnette taught Southern Baptists how to use their Sunday Schools. When he spoke, religious educators listened. We thank God for his ability to plan with vision, promote with dignity, lead with power, and preach with passion. He made us want to reach people; and, more than that, he taught us how. This unbeatable combination embodied in our leader is the ideal of each of us." Is it any wonder that God blessed the energies of such a dynamic leader who was willing to be the servant rather than the one who just presided in the huge gatherings.

The next century demands strong Sunday School leaders who will build on the legacies of those who have gone before.

The spiritual needs of the masses of people tugged at his heart, and he produced the classic commentary on compassion, *The Pull of the People*.[1] His fertile imagination sparked the idea of the "Million More in '54" campaign which moved Southern Baptists to their most glorious enlargement and evangelistic achievements.

The 21st century demands and deserves new leaders with hearts for God and a determination to get the job done in the spirit of Arthur Flake and Jasper N. Barnette.

Personal Learning Activities

1. What are the five elements of Flake's Formula? Are they relevant today? Why or why not?

2. In what ways did J. N. Barnette model servant leadership?

47

Leading the generations of the 21st century to Christ and engaging them in meaningful Bible study will depend on leaders with hearts for God and a determination to reach people for Jesus Christ.

[1]J. N. Barnette, *The Pull of the People* (Nashville: Convention Press, 1956).

Chapter 5

Jesus' Strategic Plan Will Not Change for the 21st Century

"Christian teaching is not a mere technique. It is a communication process that is centered in the person of Jesus Christ, rooted in the Word of God, and devoted to the purpose of leading individuals to life-transforming commitment."

—Lucien Coleman (1984)[1]

The years prior to the third millennium will be filled with speculations, projections, and sophisticated "crystal ball" watching. Publications, including Christian sources, will abound with trend analysis and what will be hot and what will not in the 21st century. Wild claims will be made for products, processes, and people. Entrepreneurs in all realms will profit from the phenomenon known as "propheteering." And it will be interesting to see how believers sort out the myriad of possibili-

Demands of pathfinders and pacesetters remind us that our teaching must meet needs while still presenting their first need—for Jesus Christ as Savior.

ties and also to see how, ultimately, the "cream will rise to the top."

I was invited to participate in a conference devoted to the study of boomers and busters. Speaker after speaker recited the same information about these groups of people who happened to be born in certain time periods. I listened to descriptions including:

- They want choices.
- They do not commit to anything.
- They are against institutions.

After several hours I thought to myself: *Are we discussing people or the latest virus? Who are these people really?*

My experience with individual boomers (pathfinders) and busters (pacesetters) has generally been opposite this nay-sayer approach.[2] In fact, some of the most committed people I have ever encountered were boomers and busters who had experienced a life-changing, behavior-modifying experience with Jesus, the Son of God. Everything the Lord promised in His Word completely changed the scenery for these disciples. I almost resented the fact that these dedicated believers were being thrust into the same categories as those being discussed in broad generalities in the forum.

I do admit that these are difficult days. Everywhere one turns today, he or she is faced with violence, disharmony, lack of trust, and chaos.

I remember an afternoon in Coral Gables, Florida, a community in the heart of Miami, when a church member came to my office. He served as a detective for the Miami

50

police department, and he had come to prepare the ministerial staff for what was likely to occur in our city. Miami had just experienced several riots, and major portions of the city were burned in the wake of uncontrolled violence. The detective told us a group of people in the area were extremely vicious. If they interrupted a worship service or approached the church office, we were to acquiesce to their demands immediately. This group's lack of regard for human life posed great danger for everyone.

Three events had occurred which caused the words of the Miami police officer to disturb me.

1. I had just conducted the funeral service for a young woman who happened to be at the wrong place at the wrong time.

2. A police helicopter had hovered over our home one evening, searching for criminals who had murdered two of our neighbors.

3. Our own teenage son had been attacked on the streets while bicycling home from a football practice.

During some of the sleepless nights which came after these events and the warning of the Miami detective, I pondered what was happening in our society. My thoughts took me back to a different time, a safer moment, when I was growing up as a young boy in a small community in Texas. I had just accepted Christ as my personal Savior; and one afternoon the minister of music, Fred Spann, delivered a book to me at my home. The book was *In His Steps* by Charles Sheldon. The thesis of Sheldon's book was, "What would Jesus do?"

I thought about that question in a

Understanding the needs and characteristics of adult generations equips teachers to minister to adults and their families.

51

Days are filled with violence, disharmony, lack of trust, and chaos; but Jesus is the answer. And Jesus commanded us to teach.

different manner in that darkened bedroom in Coral Gables than I had first considered it when I was a young 19 year old who had experienced little of life and had just started a journey with the Lord.

What would Jesus do? What would Jesus do in a corrupt world in the 1980s? What would Jesus do in Miami, Florida?

The answer seemed to hit me in such a way that I almost remember sitting up in bed. Yes, that was the answer! It was so obvious. If Jesus walked the streets of this beautiful, tropical city in the last part of the 20th century, He would do exactly what He did when He traveled the dusty roads of Jerusalem and Bethany.

He also lived in communities of crime and distrust. Didn't He tell a story about bandits attacking a certain person, who was later ministered to by the good Samaritan? Had the Lord not warned the disciples not to store up material goods, where moth and rust destroy and thieves break in to steal (see Matt. 6:20)? Were there not corrupt men such as Zaccheus who profited from the sorrow of his people? Did not the religious community have leaders whom Jesus classified as hypocrites? Yes. Yes. And what did the Lord do?

The answer is found in the classic book by J. M. Price, founder of the School of Religious Education at Southwestern Baptist Theological Seminary, entitled *Jesus the Teacher*.[3] He came teaching. Years later this theme was echoed again by Lucien Coleman when he published *Why the Church Must Teach*, another in-depth look at the life of Christ.

What did Jesus do when He was

52

physically on this earth? I'll tell you what He did. He taught. In fact, when Jesus faced His life's work, He chose to be a teacher. His disciples, His friends, and His enemies called Jesus Teacher. He allowed them this privilege, and He even called Himself Teacher.

I would like to ask you a question. Are there indications that the teaching ministry is regarded as a secondary and, in some instances, nonessential function of the church today? What about in your own church?

• Do the actions of your church leaders indicate how important equipping teachers is to the life of the congregation?

• If I examined your church calendar, would an emphasis on teacher training be apparent?

• Do the teachers have adequate time for lesson presentation?

• Have the leaders enlisted enough teachers to get the job done?

• What percentage of your church membership is found in weekly Bible study on any given Sunday? If you are like most churches, 50 to 75 percent of your membership is not in Bible study on Sunday morning. Their behavior indicates that they do not value studying God's Word.

I propose to you today that we must reestablish the priority of the ministry which Jesus placed foremost in His own work on earth—the ministry which was on the leading edge of the early Christian missionary movement; the ministry which, more than any other, sustained the vitality of infant churches in alien environments; the ministry of the taught Word.

Are we engaging in this significant

We must reestablish the priority of the ministry which Jesus placed foremost in His own work on earth—the ministry of teaching.

53

Today hurting people cry out for ministry, and they are hungry for God's Word.

ministry today? Is your church effective in this assignment? Does anyone even know if we are effective? Does anyone care? Do you care?

You are probably asking: "Do I care? And if I care, am I willing to do something about it?"

I recently taught in two seminaries in Brazil. The preaching ministry was flourishing in that beautiful country. During the past 25 years, Brazilian Baptists have experienced an increase in preaching points, pastors, and seminary students. But at the same time they recorded a 21 percent loss in Bible study enrollment. They are projecting another 22 percent loss by the year 2000. As I examined the records, I found that 54 out of every 100 people who professed Christ were lost to the church out the back door. The churches were not practicing the admonition of Christ to "teach them to observe all things" (see Matt. 28:19-20).

Is this God's will for His churches. I think not.

Today people are crying out for help as never before. More hurting people are open to the gospel than I have ever seen in my own ministry. Our mandate is ministry, and we are under the authority of Christ. We must be faithful to the Great Commission.

Thousands of teachers must be recruited and trained if we are to make a difference. The present teaching corps must be revitalized with passion and energy. Where will our churches find new teachers? They will come from the classes of the present teachers.

These are difficult times, but the world Jesus entered almost 2000 years ago was a

54

difficult time, too. What did He do at that time? He taught. He taught everywhere. That is exactly what you and I must do. We must be about the Father's business. That's what Jesus told his mother when He was a child. We, His children, must follow His example.

Society may crumble. We will face difficult days, perhaps violent days, just as we did that year in Miami. The church in America may be persecuted within our lifetime. Whatever happens, our marching orders are to continue to teach. The teaching ministry must be returned to its rightful place among the believers.

Reaching and teaching means that we must have trained, dedicated teachers.

Personal Learning Activities

1. What is Jesus' strategic plan? How do we know this is what He wants us to do?

2. Does your church value teaching? What evidences support your answer?

---

[1]Lucien Coleman, *Why the Church Must Teach* (Nashville: Broadman Press, 1984), 136.

[2]For a thorough discussion of adult generations, see Louis B. Hanks, *Vision, Variety, and Vitality: Teaching Today's Adult Generations* (Nashville: Convention Press, 1996).

[3]Jim Price, *Jesus the Teacher* (Nashville: The Sunday School Board of the Southern Baptist Convention, 1946).

Chapter 6

Teacher Training—Needed as Never Before

"Let the plain, painful truth be spoken. Our Sunday Schools are taught by those who know not how to teach. Our schools will never accomplish what they must do until our teachers know better how to teach and what to teach. Our teachers must themselves be taught. Whosoever shall devise the means for doing this effectually will help forward the great cause as much as if they were to put a hundred missionaries in the field."

—John S. Hart (1866)

In the 1830s, the abilities of those who taught in public schools were similar to those who taught in Sunday School. Regretfully, that cannot be stated about teachers in the two arenas today. Even though teachers in secular school systems face a certain amount of customer dissatisfaction, the distance between Sunday School and secular school has widened so far that one does not even

A century ago Sunday School teachers and public-school teachers had similar credentials and expectations. In the intervening decades the requirements for teaching in secular education have continually risen while the expectations of Sunday School teachers have continued to decrease.

consider the abilities of the average Bible study teacher to approach the abilities and training of the public-school teacher. While one has continued to add additional requirements in the form of advanced training and degree pursuits, the past 20 years has witnessed a deterioration in the level of training and competency among Bible teachers.

The paradoxical reality of this decrease in teaching skills has come during a time in which more ministers have received training and advanced academic degrees in the fields of education, age-group ministries, communications, and counseling than ever before. These equipped ministers have more choices from which to select pedagogic resources, both in print and in other media. Every day brings forth new offerings in tools which enhance learning and offer instructors the ability to make their classes come alive, both in information and in visual effects.

Once, while attending a national meeting of Southern Baptist educators, I asked this question of the more than 45 ministers of education present, "How many of you have an effective teacher improvement ministry?" To my amazement, only four raised their hands, affirming their satisfaction of the endeavor. All 45 were graduates of seminaries with master's degrees, and several had completed doctoral work. There was no lack of understanding or ability to build a program of teacher improvement. If this is happening in churches staffed by our ablest educators, what must be the plight of congregations with limited professional, ministerial assistance?

58

As discouraging as the results of that simple survey were, the group gathered there expressed little concern. As a result of professional educators' lack of attentiveness to teacher training, the condition of teaching improvement and development seems to have worsened in the years since that meeting.

Every church in the world is affected by this lackadaisical approach to quality ministry. If teachers are not continually improving and growing in the grace of the Lord, where will their students stand? If ministers of education fail to pay the price to ensure that teachers of all levels are challenged and are moving upward in their understanding of biblical truths, pupil comprehension, class ministry, and outreach, is it any wonder that evangelism is not keeping pace with population trends, especially in the southern region of the United States, once referred to as the "Bible Belt."

Southern Baptists are losing the metropolitan South. That's one conclusion from a report by Charles Chaney, Home Mission Board vice-president of extension, or church starting, who urged greater church planting efforts in Southern cities and suburbs. According to the report, the population of the United States grew 27 percent during the years studied, but the number of Southern Baptist churches increased only 13 percent.

In the South the population grew 42 percent while Southern Baptist churches increased only 9 percent. The southern population to church ratio grew from 2,196 people for every SBC church to 2,876 people.

Southern Baptists currently average

Churches have more educated, professional staff educators to train teachers than ever before in our history.

59

More types of resources—from the printed page to the computer—are available to churches to enhance teaching and learning than ever before.

1,119 church starts a year. Southern states needed 9,632 more churches at the end of 1993 for the number of people for each SBC church to equal the 1970 level.

The fact of the matter is that until today's church leaders get serious about the improvement and expansion of teaching, evangelism, church starts, and other church ministries that reach and care for people will continue to decline. J. B. Gambrell expressed it well, when he was quoted in 1900: "For years we have organized and evangelized. We have preached, but we have never taught. I believe the most significant of all modern movements is the work of teacher training."

Ninety-five years later the most significant movement which could take place as the church moves toward a third millennium would be a massive resurgence of teacher training throughout the world. Attention directed to the needs of this vital ministry would produce results from all sides.

If we turned our attention to teacher training, perhaps the first result would be that the current corps of teachers, many of whom would be considered "champions of learning," would be revitalized. Their corresponding enthusiasm would move through the membership much like a roaring river. No one has more influence than the Bible teacher, especially those who have proved themselves through years of experience and dedicated service.

The Bible teacher is in many ways the most trusted person in the church. The following story demonstrates what I mean.

Throughout my ministry in churches

60

I have often asked members, "Who is the treasurer of the church?"

After they give me the name of the treasurer, I ask, "Do you trust this person?"

Their immediate response is always a resounding yes!

Then I ask, "Do you ever ask the treasurer to bring a report to the congregation concerning how the tithes and offerings are disbursed?"

Of course, regular reports are always provided to the members regarding this important task.

I counter their affirmation by a simple: "I thought you trusted the treasurer. Why do you demand a regular reporting system?"

They always respond with laughter because it is ridiculous even to imagine placing a person in a position with so much responsibility and not exacting a heavy degree of accountability—accountability which benefits both parties.

Yet that is exactly what most churches do with their teachers. Teachers are assigned a major role in the ministry of the congregation, provided a group of learners, and often provided a free rein on instruction. Many times pastors and other church leaders do not even know what doctrines are taught or what attitudes are displayed behind those closed doors of learning.

Without doubt the teacher is the most trusted person in the congregation. Church members can thank the Lord for the teachers of our churches and the trust they have earned through their devotion to the Lord and to the faithful teaching of God's Word.

From 1970 to 1993, the ratio of population in southern states to SBC churches moved from 2,196 persons for every SBC church to 2,876 persons per SBC church.

61

"I believe the most significant of all modern movements is the work of teacher training."
—J. B. Gambrell

Dedication to the improvement of teacher training would probably profit the experienced teacher even more than the novice. I make that statement, knowing that most believe that new recruits need more assistance than experienced teachers. I disagree.

My own experience with teachers in Southern Baptist congregations has caused me more concern with those experienced teachers who have grand respect from their constituents. These teachers often have the ability to respond to a quick call to present a Bible study which causes the listener to be amazed at the extent of Bible knowledge and the dexterity of delivery. Usually, when the discourse is finished, everyone believes the teacher has stepped up to the plate and knocked the ball completely out of the park.

The only problem is that while those listeners look on the outside the Lord sees the heart (see 1 Sam. 16:7). If the experienced teacher has not continued in his or her walk with the Lord and worked to continue to improve teaching skills, the only one not blessed by such a moment may be the teacher. We do a disservice to our long-serving, experienced teachers when we do not keep their weapons sharpened and their creative thoughts challenged.

I once heard Claude Thomas, pastor of First Baptist Church, Euless, Texas, make this statement to a group of pastors and religious educators, "To a learner, everyone is a teacher." An effective teacher is also continually learning, and everyone can be and is a teacher.

In spite of the obvious need for

62

teacher training, churches seem to ignore the need or to struggle with it. Here are two reasons most teacher training programs do not work:

1. Ministers of education, Sunday School directors, and age-group division directors are often intimidated by teachers who have taught for years and have gained the respect of the entire congregation. I distinctly remember a competent Sunday School director telling me, "Oh, I could never lead a Sunday School workers weekly planning meeting because Dr. 'So-in-So' knows more about the Scriptures than I could ever know."

2. Often those same staff members and general officers feel that revered and experienced teachers probably would not profit from attending such a meeting. This attitude leads experienced teachers to absent themselves from such a training session, thereby crippling the process in two ways.

Experienced teachers need ongoing training just as newly appointed teachers do.

• The example of the experienced teachers' lack of participation sends signals to teachers who desperately need this learning experience that the meeting is probably not worth attending because the best teachers in the church do not recognize its value. This continues to lower the standard of teaching throughout the Bible study organization and denies both the novice and the expert the privilege of mentoring and learning from those who have been down that road before.

• The Bible continues to warn believers not to "think too highly of themselves" (see Rom. 12:3) and to consider their own walk, lest they be tempted. Galatians 6:7-10 says: "Be not deceived; God is not mocked: for whatsoever a

63

No one has more influence than the Bible teacher.

man soweth, that shall he also reap. For he that soweth to his flesh shall of the flesh reap corruption; but he that soweth to the Spirit shall of the Spirit reap life everlasting. And let us not be weary in well doing: for in due season we shall reap, if we faint not. As we have therefore opportunity, let us do good unto all men, especially unto them who are of the household of faith."

Teachers who purposefully reject the leadership provided by their pastor, minister of education, Sunday School director, or division or department director will ultimately lose a dimension of their own leadership. It may not be readily apparent, but in time a terrible toll will be paid.

A stream always succeeds in forging its own way to the ocean, overcoming all obstacles in its path. With vision and perseverance, so, too, can we achieve our desired success.

Christian educators have a responsibility of care and concern for the overall health of today's Bible teachers. These teachers deserve the best in teacher training, and they also deserve leaders who will challenge them to levels of performance they dare not attempt alone.

If you want to make a difference in the lives of people, pour yourselves into the lives and ministries of the Bible teachers of your church.

John Hart's words were right on target in 1866, and his words ring even truer today than they did in the middle of the 19th century. "Whosoever shall devise the means for doing this effectually will help forward the great cause as much as if they were to put a

64

hundred missionaries in the field."

Personally, I believe teachers are waiting to be challenged to another level. Whether they are champions or have just been enlisted, teachers need ongoing training. The Bible study leader who steps forward to challenge teachers of all levels will make a difference in this generation which will be difficult to match in any century.

Personal Learning Activities

1. Does your church adequately train its teachers by providing ongoing opportunities for training? What statements in this chapter apply to your church?

2. Do you expect experienced teachers to continue to train? Why or why not?

The teacher is the most trusted person in the congregation.

65

Chapter 7

Leadership Training—You Can Do It

"**W**e must remember that one person is much the same as another, and that those are best who are trained."

—**Thucydides (404 B.C.)**

I remember the moment as if it were yesterday. We sat in a car, parked across the campus from the University of Miami. Feeling a sense of shame and an uneasiness about broaching the subject, finally I was able to express what I had been wanting to tell my former seminary teacher all week long. He did not seem shocked or surprised.

As I had done in previous churches, I always invited Jack Terry, dean of the School of Religious Education at Southwestern Baptist Theological Seminary, to lead a teaching workshop at the churches I served. My journey through the University Baptist Church in Coral Gables, Florida, was not an exception. Jack had been asked to provide leadership; and, as usual, he was "knocking a home run" with our teachers.

He seemed to glide through his helpful presentations on

67

> "Live your life so that your children can tell their children that you not only stood for something wonderful—you acted on it."
> —Dan Zadra

the art of teaching; and I felt a tinge of envy, secretly wishing that I possessed such skills. The people seemed to hang on to each word he said, and they readily accepted his how-to illustrations.

Finally, after several previous attempts, I confided to my friend my own sense of futility, especially in the realm of teaching improvement. "I am actually afraid of the faculty meetings, and I almost dread the arrival of Wednesday evenings," I said. "I have always had a lisp, and often I find myself stumbling over some of the more difficult biblical names."

I finally exclaimed, "Jack, I am miserable; and I don't know what to do!"

He paused before answering; and I sensed that he was purposefully thinking through his response, not wanting to inflict further pain to one who obviously needed no additional burdens.

"Bill, you are 40 years old. Why don't you do what you enjoy doing. You are an excellent promoter and encourager. Your skills in administration of a solid Sunday School organization are good, and your people skills are well accepted by the congregation. Don't worry about this area which seems to threaten you. Other people like me have given their lives to mastering these skills, and you can use them. In fact, Bill, when can we book a return engagement for me to come back to University Baptist?"

His words were like good news from a far country. I was delighted to hear his response. It brought me an instant feeling of relief. I immediately accepted his solution; and

68

with a merry heart we journeyed toward the church site, arriving in time for the evening session.

I was able to live with that decision for about three months. Finally, I felt so convicted by what I think was the Spirit of God, that I could no longer hide behind Jack's well-meaning directive. I had to address this weakness, and I marched into the Wednesday night faculty training session and boldly took over the leadership role.

Suddenly Wednesday evenings became what I longed for them to be. I prepared daily. Faculty meetings became the most enjoyable experience of my week.

The teachers at University Baptist responded in a marvelous way, many times completely packing out the remodeled chapel where we met. Often we approached 100 percent in leadership participation.

I discovered that when I opened up to the Sunday School leaders, with all of my weaknesses, they opened up to me. A bond was created which basically said, "If Bill is willing to chance it, why shouldn't we."

Later, when I became the minister of education at the young Prestonwood Baptist Church in Dallas, Texas, I continued my emphasis on leadership development. I remember the first night we met. We placed chairs along the hallway, in groups of three and four, and immediately jumped into getting the job done.

The frenetic schedule of this rapidly growing congregation placed such a time limitation on me that often I felt uneasy about my own personal preparation for the meetings. Several

Spectacular achievements are always preceded by unspectacular preparations.

69

> "The man who is prepared has his battle half fought."
> —Cervantes

times my entire day was spent with a crew of architects. I would finish working with them just in time to grab my teaching resources for a quick review and then walk in to lead an eager group of teachers. And yet the room would be packed with eager learners, excited about the possibilities of meeting with their classes next Sunday for Bible study.

Circumstances made it possible for me, in 1985, to employ Jack Terry as teaching specialist/instructor for the Prestonwood Baptist Church. His assignment was to lead teacher training sessions on Wednesdays and Sundays.

I was ecstatic, and the people were excited. Terry did his usual stellar job, presenting weekly information which was probably the finest in the world. Teachers received additional commentary, specially prepared by Terry; and he was always available to answer their questions. He proved to be a great partner in ministry.

But the results of Terry's involvement took an interesting turn. A major responsibility of ministers of education, Sunday School directors, and age-group division and department directors is to monitor participation rates and trends. As I monitored this at Prestonwood, I saw that, though the rate of attendance was acceptable, it never kept pace with the attendance when I, as the minister of education, was the chief instructor.

I could not understand the trend line:

• The teachers were being led by one of the finest educators in the world.

• This educator devoted large amounts of his

70

time to make sure the best learning environment was provided each week.

• The actual learning experience was charged each week with excitement and joy.

• The additional resources provided, along with those included in the curriculum materials from the Sunday School Board, were top-notch.

Knowing that this gifted Christian educator was providing the faculty members of the Sunday School perhaps 100 percent more than they ever received from my instructions, why did more attend when the sessions were led by their own minister of education? The answer became crystal clear at the precise moment I mentally formed the question. I was their minister of education. I was the one who had prayed with them and enlisted them for service. They felt accountable to me because I was their leader. When I had informed them that they were to be present in the faculty training period and that I would be leading those sessions, they responded.

They loved Jack Terry; but he represented specialized instruction, not leader-follower relationships. This was a resplendent moment for me because I realized that Sunday School teachers and workers do not have to have the expert present for a meaningful learning experience to occur—one that will strengthen the teaching corps of the churches. Bible study leaders of the churches stand ready to follow their own leaders.

This is good news for professors and local-church ministers. There are not enough Jack Terrys to lead all our churches in teacher training and ongoing workers planning times.

When leaders open up to teachers, teachers respond with openness, excitement, and faithfulness.

71

No one can provide better leadership for teachers than their own leaders.

The professors multiply themselves through the students they equip and send out to lead the churches. This process affirms the professors, equips the ministers, and gives leadership to the churches.

I hope this story has caused you to rethink weekly workers meetings in your own church. No one can provide better help for your Bible study teachers than your Sunday School director and minister of education, if your church has professional educators on staff. All teachers and workers benefit from training together. A bond is formed that builds relationships, keeps everyone accountable, and offers all involved an opportunity to grow in skill development and their walk with the Lord.

If you are a minister of education, a Sunday School director, a division or department director, believe in yourself. Dare to walk into the arena which may represent a challenge to you. You will find that teachers of all levels eagerly wait to join you in the quest of being the best teachers possible for our Lord, the Master Teacher.

Personal Learning Activities

1. What is the relationship between those who lead weekly planning meetings and teachers? How can this relationship be improved?

2. If you have a role in these weekly sessions, in what ways do you feel inadequate? What steps can you take to improve your skills or to provide additional training from experts.

72

Chapter 8
Weak Preparation

"There are Baptists who believe the Bible literally, use it devotionally, but don't take it seriously. Most of us have embraced a discipleship that trivializes the gospel."

—Tom Sine

During a church consultation I was startled by the comments of one of the more able children's teachers: "If the parents of this church knew how poor the level of teaching is that their children are receiving each Sunday, there would be a revolt taking place in the offices of the pastor and the minister of education." She had taken a brief leave of absence from her regularly assigned department and was serving as a substitute in several of the preschool and children's departments.

The worker continued: "I am amazed that these parents, who represent the best in the business arena, are pacified into thinking that learning is taking place just because the workers give them a paper with a Bible verse that their child has colored. Hardly any preparation is made, just some quick remedy requiring little effort from the worker. The parents know what is going on in the public classroom, but they make a mistake in not attempting to investigate what is happening at their church."

Sadly, this scene is being played out in churches all over

73

Quality Christian education demands a commitment to weekly preparation at all levels including the pastor, the minister of education, division and department directors, teachers, and class participants.

America. Not only have many of our churches reverted to baby-sitting as opposed to an active learning environment for their children, but also many parents and pastors do not even know that the situations are occurring.

This is not a condemnation of any one particular discipline. In fact, all who have had anything to do with Christian education in the past 20 years must bear responsibility for this dilemma. Many factors are included in this mix, and all have spurred this deterioration in the learning opportunities:

• Pastors who have not taken the time to know the true condition of their education ministries.

• Education ministers who have allowed the training processes of leadership to decay.

• Adult teachers who have not prepared members to provide the leadership base which is required for good teacher-student ratios.

• Personnel and nominating committees who have not set forth standards of performance necessary to meet members' needs.

• Parents who have not taken the time to stay informed about what their children are doing on Sunday morning.

• Members who have not demanded that deficiencies be addressed in a manner which honors the admonitions of the Lord.

I recall a conversation I had with a friend who worked in the Advanced Training Center for the IBM Corporation. He said that there was a time when IBM hardly had to market their products because they were in such demand. If you wanted a Selectric typewriter, there was a three- to six-month waiting period.

74

During this period the sales division at Big Blue grew soft; and when personal computers hit the streets, IBM was slow to address the needs of the customer.

In many churches fewer people attend Sunday School than at a previous time in the church's history. Have church leaders missed what members really want and need? Have we tried too hard to fill positions that we have lowered our standards to say we have no teacher vacancies? Have we thought that because positions were filled and we heard no complaints that we were doing a good job?

Could the answer be that Southern Baptists forgot that people learn slowly and forget quickly. Principles of learning and workshops related to pedagogy require continuous repetition. Leaders have a responsibility to remind current teachers consistently of teaching skills and student needs. And teachers benefit from continual motivation; or they will move toward the easy way out or forget important, basic skills.

Nothing can ever be assumed concerning new leaders. The most attentive directions must always be given to new teachers, reinforcing and encouraging along the path, making sure they are fully equipped for the great tasks ahead.

After my encounter with the frustrated children's worker, I started asking myself probing questions concerning my own commitment to the value of Christian education and discipleship.

• Would I be pleased if my church used

"It is always with the best intention that the worst work is done."
—Oscar Wilde

75

Athletes have muscle, speed, and skills. They excel for one reason—preparation. Bible teachers can offer the same level of preparedness on Sunday morning.

resources which were weak in Bible content and masked the gospel?

• Would I be pleased if my church used resources that had limited teaching foundations concerning the Great Commission?

• Would I be pleased if I knew the amount of time the average teacher in my church spent in weekly preparation?

• Would I be pleased if my church provided the best learning opportunities possible for all ages, especially children and youth?

Then the questions became more personal. I have two grandsons, ages three and one. Of course, I want the best for them. In fact, I would be less than what a grandfather should be if I did not do everything in my realm of influence to ensure that all children are taught from their infancy. My pondering caused me to ask, "Are they getting quality education from prepared teachers in their Sunday School?"

How do you measure effective teaching in your Sunday School?

• Do you evaluate resources for content, educational level and value, application and relevance, adherence to God's Word?

• Do you observe to see if participants are actively engaged in learning?

• Do you offer teachers ideas, training, and motivation on a weekly basis and at other times convenient to their schedules?

• Are training sessions you offer worthy of participants' time and commitment?

The 20th century has been characterized by a devotion to sports of every description. Today the seasons of play actually run into one another and encroach on what was previously

76

believed to be another sport's domain. We watch basketball into the baseball season, and then baseball conflicts with the third month of the football season. For the athlete, there is no off season anymore.

One truth has come forth from this profusion of athletic events: The difference between these titans of muscle, speed, and skills is one quality—preparation. Whether it is the local high-school coach poring over last Friday night's game film, getting ready for the practice sessions on Monday or the professional manager, assisted by computers, who can forecast what the tendencies of the opposing pitchers and batters will be, the implications are the same. In an arena where the difference in winning and losing is often measured in nanoseconds, preparation proves to be the key to success.

If athletes are willing to pay the price in personal preparation in order to attain a title, which soon is forgotten and relegated to some trivial statistic in the future, how much more diligence must be brought forth by those whose charges make a difference in the eternal consequences of people. Never let it be said that a sports personality, who often does not even know the Lord as personal Savior, is willing to rise to a level of preparation and performance which causes Bible study leaders to bow their heads in shame because their expectations and willingness to put forth their best efforts pale in comparison. This should not be so!

Excellence starts with one Bible study leader. Today you can be the one who moves to a higher plane, encouraging others to follow your example. Our preschoolers, chil-

"There is nothing harder than the softness of indifference."
—Juan Montalvo

77

A Sunday School teacher's weekly preparedness has eternal consequences.

dren, youth, and adults deserve your best in service to the Master Teacher.

Personal Learning Activities

1. Do you, as a leader of the Sunday School, know the quality of teaching taking place in each age group of your Sunday School? What criteria will you use to determine effectiveness?

2. Excellence comes from prepared, committed, trained leaders. How can you help your church stay on the cutting edge of its performance standard?

Chapter 9

Can You See It? Believing Is Seeing

"Some things have to be believed to be seen."

The Word of God is filled with poignant moments, especially in the life of our Lord, Jesus Christ. The disciples were forever on the brink of something they never expected. Some of the times were dramatic, such as the night Jesus walked on the sea. At other times this inner group of believers shared reflective experiences. Occasionally, dramatic events happened in the midst of throngs of people crowding to get closer to Jesus.

The moments that have fascinated me most deal with the perspective Jesus placed on common events. We also learn much about Jesus by simple remarks made by the New Testament writers. We sometimes miss these comments because our attention is drawn to another part of the event which seems to us to be more significant.

Matthew recorded one of those moments when he described what we commonly refer to as the Sermon on the Mount: "And when He saw the multitudes" (Matt. 5:1, NASB).[1] Our immediate attention is drawn to the fact that "He went up on the mountain,

"And seeing the multitudes, He felt compassion for them."
—Matthew 9:36, NASB

and after He sat down, His disciples came to Him." That is the action; now we are on the edge of our seat, awaiting whatever the Lord may do next. And, no doubt, the marvelous teaching that came forth is certainly the heart of the life of believers as we attempt to be light and salt in a desperate generation. But Matthew thought it was important to write, "He saw. . . ."

Another passage I love is the beautiful picture of New Testament evangelism found in John 1:38: "And Jesus turned, and beheld them following" (NASB). One of the two disciples of John the Baptist who followed the Lord was Andrew. He immediately went to his brother, Simon Peter, and also to Philip. After meeting Jesus, Philip found Nathanael and said, "We have found Him of whom Moses in the Law and also the Prophets wrote, Jesus of Nazareth, the son of Joseph" (John 1:45, NASB).

Nathanael's cryptic response provides insight into his life and is one of the most famous passages in the New Testament, "Can any good thing come out of Nazareth?" (John 1:46, NASB).

Philip passed his first test of witness training when he chose not to argue but rather implored Nathanael to "come and see" (John 1:46, NASB).

The resulting encounter is exciting. Jesus said of him, "Behold, an Israelite indeed, in whom is no guile" (John 1:47, NASB).

Nathanael boldly asked him how He knew him. At this point we find another simple statement: "Before Philip called you, . . . I saw you" (John 1:48, NASB).

Turning back to Matthew, we find a

80

story recording the rigorous pace of the Lord: "And Jesus was going about all the cities and the villages, teaching in their synagogues and proclaiming the gospel of the kingdom, and healing every kind of disease and every kind of sickness" (Matt. 9:35, NASB). Then out of the clear, we feel the love of God, "And seeing the multitudes, He felt compassion for them" (Matt. 9:36, NASB).

Wow! In the middle of this frenetic schedule, a simple phrase appears—"*seeing the multitudes.*" I do not think it is just by happenstance that the disciples were taught their first lesson in leadership enlistment. Those who would ultimately be able to share the good news around the world learned from Jesus.

The closing portion of the Gospel of John touches my heart as I read that Jesus, while dying on the cross, "saw His mother and the disciple whom He loved" (John 19:36, NASB). In the midst of giving His life on the cross, the Lord was aware of human need. Hallelujah! What a Savior!

This accounting of just a few incidences in the life of Christ points out that Jesus was constantly aware of needs around Him. Whether in a crowd or in a small group of disciples, Jesus saw. . . . Creating a better future starts with the ability to envision it.

I once had the privilege of working with a pastor who challenged me in many ways during the time we served together. Although we had many staff meetings and personal encounters during those days of ministry, he placed one exhortation before me on a daily basis.

"The harvest is plentiful, but the workers are few. Therefore, beseech the Lord of the harvest to send out workers into His harvest."
—Matthew 9:37-38, NASB

To meet the needs of hurting people in our midst, we must keep our eyes on Jesus and care for others as He did.

The pastor would say to me: "Bill, can you see it? Can you see God building a great army of believers in our community? Can you see thousands of people accepting Christ as their personal Savior? Can you see God using you to enlist and train hundreds of leaders and teachers for Bible study ministry? Can you see the Lord building His church, which will storm the gates of hell?"

Then my pastor would pause. Sometimes I felt as if he were looking into my being. Then he would say, "Bill, if you cannot see it before you see it, you will never see it."

Today I am excited because I have been privileged to see God move in ways that seem miraculous in our sight. I thank God for that pastor's insightful urging me to be aware of the great opportunities to "be about the Father's business" (see Luke 2:49).

My question to you is, Are you able to see as Jesus saw? Our world is filled with more people than ever before, and the needs of our society are greater than at any other time in history. When you see the teeming masses, are you moved with compassion? Are you willing to be God's disciple to do something which will make a difference in the lives of people throughout the world.

A comedian once said, "You know there are people out there because you see them when you look at them." Churches often have a tendency to look at people, but the hard-driving question is, Do they see them?

Several years ago I was asked by the president of the Southern Baptist Religious Education Association, Bob Edd Shotwell, to

82

make a presentation to its annual meeting. Bob Ed asked me to center the speech around the theme, Navigating the Nineties. It was to be a study of accomplishments of the past and present and a forecast of what the 90s might hold for religious educators.

The Sunday School Board provided informational data which I used in making my report. As I examined the materials, I was shocked at what I read. In 1989, 8,003 Southern Baptist churches did not baptize one person.

Reaching and teaching go hand in hand.

I remember how my mind suddenly started calculating what it meant for 8,003 churches not to experience new life in a 52-week period. My calculations were as follows:

• 7,003 pastors could not lead one person to Christ. (I reduced the number of churches by one thousand, thinking that perhaps that many churches were pastorless in 1989.)

• If each of these churches had only three deacons, 24,009 deacons did not lead one person to saving knowledge of the Lord.

• If each of these churches had 10 Sunday School teachers, 80,030 Bible teachers could not lead one person to the Lord during a time duration of 365 days.

• If the average attendance of the 8,003 churches was 50 members per Sunday, 400,150 believers could not even lead one relative to the Lord.

Further examination of Southern Baptist statistics for 1989 revealed that the Sunday School attendance had dropped over 50,000 per week. These were startling statistics; yet when I shared them in my speech, I got little response.

83

Caring about those without Christ means taking the time to get involved in their lives.

I wondered to myself, *If a company had more than eight thousand dealerships which did not make one sale all year and if the bottom line had plummeted below profitable margins, do you think that someone might have brought this up at the annual meeting?*

Speakers often pepper their presentations with cliches such as, "They do not care how much you know, until they know how much you care." Is it possible that people without Christ know Christians who are so busy with their own agendas and schedules that they do not see the people around them in need of a Savior?

I recently talked to a professor who told me that she had been assigned to accompany a guest speaker to the platform at a recent chapel program. Seated in the auditorium, she was experiencing an amiable conversation with the visiting scholar when suddenly the president of the school entered the room, greeting the guest with the following statement, "Oh, they have left you alone." Not only did he not speak to the professor, but his actions also implied that he did not even acknowledge her presence. Trying to shield her embarrassment and understandable hurt, she laughingly told me that she wanted to ask, "Did I put on my invisible suit today?"

I personally know all the parties involved in the preceding story, and the inexcusable actions on the part of the president were not premeditated. In fact, he would be as bruised if confronted with his insensitivity as the professor was with being treated as a nonperson. He just was not aware of her presence. He saw her,

84

but he did not see her. His position as the leader of the institution and the role he played as the professor's boss made the pain even more intense.

If church leaders are going to penetrate the 21st century, they are going to have to address this shortcoming. It happens on every level and at every size of church. No one is exempt from unkind behavior, which not only causes discomfort but also blocks opportunities for growth and future relationships.

Usually before they were aware of His presence, Jesus saw them. He saw them and had compassion for them, and taught them, and ministered to their needs. He challenged them to their best. And He loved them before they loved him.

The words of an old hymn are always appropriate in any age:

> Open my eyes, that I may see
> Glimpses of truth thou hast for me;
> Place in my hand the wonderful key
> That shall unclasp and set me free:
>
> Silently now I wait for Thee,
> Ready my God, thy Will to see;
> Open my eyes, illumine me,
> Spirit divine.
> —Clara H. Scott

Do you know that they are out there because when you look at them you see them?

Personal Learning Activities

1. In the Scripture passages cited here, whom did Jesus see?

"*Modo et modo non habebant modum.*" (By and by never comes.) —St. Augustine

85

2. What did the pastor mean when he said, "If you cannot see it before you see it, you will never see it"?

[1]From the *New American Standard Bible.* © The Lockman Foundation, 1960, 1962, 1963, 1968, 1971, 1972, 1973, 1975, 1977. Used by permission. Subsequent quotations marked NASB.

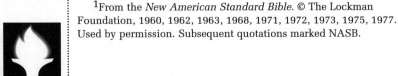

Jesus saw people before they saw Him, and He loved them.

86

Chapter 10

A New Paradigm for Sunday School?

"Lord, give me a sharp sense of understanding, a retentive memory, and the ability to grasp things correctly and fundamentally. Grant me the talent of being exact in my explanations, and the ability to express myself with thoroughness and charm. Point out the beginning, direct the progress, and help in the completion."

—Thomas Aquinas

One of the fascinating benefits of serving Southern Baptist churches is having the opportunity to spend lengthy amounts of time with pastors. These servants live under the constant pressure of preparing between three and five sermons weekly. The congregations which listen to these sermons record in their Bibles and journals the dates when various texts are used and often include the illustrations. This practice intensifies the pressure of the presenter to be continually fresh. The pastor who preaches the same sermon or uses the same illustration too often is certain to hear about it from meticulous, note-taking members.

87

> "The paradigm is the way we perceive the world."
> —Adam Smith

This weekly assignment often causes a glaze in the preacher's eye. He must continually search for new ideas, new illustrations, and new words which enhance communication.

Perry Sanders, pastor of First Baptist Church, Lafayette, Louisiana, is a prime example of this "freshness syndrome." Perry, Jr., his son, is a talented lawyer; and the two often engaged in verbal battle to see who could find a new phrase or new word which was not in the working vocabulary of the other. When Sanders, Sr., discovered a new word, the staff would be the first recipients of his surreptitious elocution.

Several years ago, when I was preparing for a presentation to the Southern Baptist Religious Education Association, I heard for the first time a word which has since become popular. The word is *paradigm*; and I first heard it from Joel Barker, a business consultant who specialized in trend development for Fortune 500 companies.

Barker's famous story about the watch industry was making the rounds at that time. He explained that the electronic quartz movement was invented by Swiss engineers in their research institute in Neuchatel, Switzerland. The Swiss leaders did not recognize its value and, through neglect, ultimately lost the benefit of the quartz technology to the Japanese and also over 60 percent of its worldwide market share in the watch-making industry.

Barker said: "The irony of this story for the Swiss is that the situation was totally avoidable if only the Swiss watch manufacturers had known how to think about their own future. If only they had known the kind of change they

88

were facing—a paradigm shift."

Leaders from the business and church world clasped on to this word *paradigm.* Businesses started making immediate application to their shrinking financial position, and denominations referred to declining or plateauing churches. Books started hitting the press, and every leadership conference in the world made sure that the word *paradigm* was planted somewhere within the conference promotional materials.

After several years of listening to this constant bombardment on the basic core of ministry of the churches in America, I have come to the conclusion that somewhere between the two extremes lies the answer—discarding what is currently used and going to a new pattern of operations or clinging to the institutional approach to its dying demise.

During the 1995 Southern Baptist Convention in Atlanta, Georgia, I was having breakfast in the hotel prior to the morning session. The restaurant was designed and located within the building in such a way as to allow me to see many parts of the hotel. The registration/reservations area was on the first floor near the elevator, yet I could see people walking on the upper floors. The concierge desk was nearby, and a small coffee shop was nestled under an umbrella close to the escalator.

I thought: I *am witnessing a beautiful example of a process of meeting the needs of the customers of this hotel. It is not necessarily a new paradigm, but it is a completed process.*

I considered the following:
- The hostess greeted our party warmly and

T-ogether
E-verybody
A-chieves
M-ore

—Mike Ditka

89

> "A paradigm is the basic way of perceiving, thinking, valuing, and doing associated with a particular vision of reality."
> —Willis Harmon

ushered us to our assigned table.

- Someone had made sure the table was clean and was set for the next customer.
- The hostess informed us that a person named Kelly would be our waiter.
- Kelly arrived soon afterwards, taking our order for coffee and juice immediately.
- He pointed out the items on the menu, recommending certain possibilities which he thought were outstanding.
- Only a brief period after he had taken our orders, he promptly brought to our table a sumptuous breakfast. He did not leave our table until he was assured that everything had met our expectations.
- Later Kelly brought the check and politely encouraged us to have a wonderful day.

During this time, while Kelly and the hostess were assisting our party, the following activities were taking place:

- A bellman was greeting a family which had just arrived from North Carolina.
- A security officer was noticeably present in the driveway.
- Another employee was checking the family's car into valet parking.
- The baggage of the vacationing family was being loaded on a cart for transportation to their assigned room.
- Another family was given a receipt for their car which had been parked.
- Two hotel employees were assisting a young couple as they departed.
- Five people had been assigned to the registration desk, assisting more than 20 people at one time.

90

• Three other employees were checking customers out of the hotel.

• Maids on the upper floors were meticulously cleaning the rooms.

• The hum of vacuum cleaners could be heard in the hallways.

• Maintenance personnel were attending to problems reported by customers.

• New hotel employees were being trained by the human resources department.

• A man in the business office was completing a contract for a convention which would meet in the Atlanta hotel in 1997.

• The chief executive officer of the hotel was listening to a proposal from a computer vendor who was explaining how much more effective the operation could be if a certain brand of software were installed.

• The marketing department was putting the final touches on a new promotional brochure which would be mailed to customers around the world. The final proof for the ad copy for the airline magazines was to be finished that week also.

• A vacationing family of four was receiving instructions about the best places to visit in Atlanta from the employees located in the concierge area.

• A businessman from Chicago was purchasing the morning paper at the gift shop.

• A vendor was assisting an employee in the gift shop to determine the amount of sundry items the hotel should purchase during the next month.

• A chef was preparing the hotel's specialty, strawberry crepes.

The answer for churches lies somewhere between discarding what is currently used to go to a new pattern of operations and clinging to the institutional approach to its dying demise.

91

• An assistant was washing vegetables which would be a part of the luncheon menu.

• A worker was sending the dishes through specialized washing procedures, ensuring that the items were clean and that the water was the proper temperature for sterilization.

All of this activity was taking place while I was enjoying the company of friends at a small restaurant which was a part of the process of the hotel system in which I was a customer. It was a process, not a paradigm. And if any part of that process failed, the following would result:

• Messy rooms
• Discourteous employees
• Unfair business practices
• Unjustified hotel charges
• A damaged automobile
• An unsafe environment
• An unclean fork

No amount of brightly colored brochures, touting the advantages of the hotel, could have salvaged the experience.

Barker gives the following definitions of paradigm:

• Thomas S. Kuhn said, "Paradigms provide models from which spring particular coherent traditions of scientific research." (*The Structure of Scientific Revolutions*)

• Adam Smith said: "The paradigm is the way we perceive the world. . . . It explains the world to us and helps us to predict its behavior." (*Powers of the Mind*)

• Willis Harmon said, "A paradigm is the basic way of perceiving, thinking, valuing, and doing associated with a particular vision of reality." (*An Incomplete Guide to the Future*)

92

• Marilyn Ferguson said, "A paradigm is a framework of thought . . . a scheme for understanding and explaining certain aspects of reality." (*The Aquarian Conspiracy*)

• Barker's own definition is, "A paradigm is a set of rules and regulations that does two things: (1) it establishes or defines boundaries; and (2) it tells you how to behave inside the boundaries in order to be successful."

Hotels use different paradigms:

• The Hyatt and Doubleday hotels cater to the upper end of the market. People are willing to pay for the extras.

• Embassy Suites and Regency Inns have targeted business travelers who need more space and can use a kitchen during extended stays.

• The Hampton Inn has led the way in providing complimentary breakfasts.

• Motel 6 claims that guests will receive a clean room at a great price.

Regardless of their accepted paradigm, none would succeed in business if their operational process broke down.

I propose to you that the average congregation does not necessarily need a new paradigm as much as it needs to examine its current process of ministry.

The classic book *The Church Organized and Functioning* reminds readers that it is one thing to organize but an entirely different matter to make sure the organization functions in the prescribed manner for which it was designed.

During an average church year, do the following processes function according to design:

"A paradigm is a framework of thought . . . a scheme for understanding and explaining certain aspects of reality."
—Marilyn Ferguson

93

"A paradigm is a set of rules and regulations that does two things: (1) it establishes or defines boundaries; and (2) it tells you how to behave inside the boundaries in order to be successful."
—Joel Barker

• Do all portions of the evangelism and outreach ministry function in such a way that no one is ever overlooked?

• Does the new member assimilation process encourage full participation from those whom it has reached?

• Are clear directions given to all members concerning discipleship growth paths?

• Is it obvious to all members how to get involved in ministry and where their gifts can best be used?

• Are expectations clearly understood about possibilities, stewardship, leadership opportunities, etc.?

• Are classes and departments organized and functioning to make sure the needs of all members and prospects are fully met?

I was following a truck down Old Hickory Boulevard in Nashville, Tennessee. The prominent sign on the side of the truck carried the following message, VIP. I immediately thought of *very important person*. I was wrong. In this particular case it meant "very important projects."

As I drove on to my home, I changed the meaning: VIP—very important process. It really does not matter what paradigm is put forward. A church must see that ministry actions and other tasks are done in the Spirit of Christ. The biblical exhortation that "all things be done decently and in order" is apropos for this conclusion (see 1 Cor. 14:40).

If the secular business environment is concerned enough about its customers to make sure every assignment is properly executed, how much more diligence and attention to

94

detail should be the pattern of ministry to those who serve the living Lord?

Personal Learning Activities

1. Choose one of the definitions of paradigm and apply it to the church.

2. Read again the paradigms of the various hotel chains. What is distinctive about your church? What is its paradigm?

The Bible admonishes us to do all things "decently and in order." That includes all aspects of a church's Bible Teaching-Reaching Ministry.

Chapter 11
Give Sunday School Back to Robert Raikes

"**W**ell done is better than well said."

—Benjamin Franklin

One of the key distinctives about the Sunday School movement is that it was created by laypersons; developed by Sunday School pioneers who were laypersons; and under the leadership of the laity, experienced its greatest period of growth.

Historians are divided as to who first started Bible study ministries, which became known as Sunday Schools. But everyone agrees that a young English businessman, moved by the plight of children in Gloschester, must be acknowledged as one who should receive a major portion of the credit.

Some say the first modern Sunday School was established in Gloucester, England, in 1780, by Robert Raikes. His work among prisoners convinced him that religious education would help keep young people out of jail. Because so many children worked in factories every day except Sunday, he formed a school that met on

97

Attention to minute organizational details ensured that the Sunday School would stay focused on people.

Sundays in the homes of lay teachers. The movement spread rapidly in England and Wales and was introduced in 1785 in the United States.

The involvement of businessmen and other laypersons proved to be an asset to the young movement. The organizational skills of businessmen provided a structure for Sunday School, which ensured its success. The attention to minute details meant that nothing would be left to chance, and particular care would be appropriated at all times. This ultimately meant that there would be no loss of energy or direction, meaning that people became and remained priority.

Students of the Sunday School movement know that the early days were difficult as beachheads were established in Christendom for this new approach in ministry. The clergy was particularly skeptical of the place of this emphasis.

Early criticisms of the Sunday School movement were:
- It desecrated the Lord's day.
- It was a new means of salvation.
- It was a secular organization.
- It discriminated against the rich.

Recently, I was asked to make a presentation to the Second Baptist Church of Richmond, Virginia, in acknowledgment of 175 years of continuous Bible study through the Sunday School organization. I presented a plaque from the Sunday School Board; and I, in turn, received a gift—a book, chronicling the entire history of Second Baptist.

As I read the book, I discovered that Second Baptist Church was organized because

98

its founding members had dared to conduct a Sunday School class in the balcony of the old Richmond Baptist Church, later to be named the First Baptist Church of Richmond.

In 1816, two dedicated young men, David Roper, a minister, and William Crane, a merchant, decided to organize a Sunday School. David was the superintendent, and the school started with four teachers and six pupils.

John Courtney served as pastor, and he was not enthralled by this new means of discipleship. Known to his congregation as "Father Courtney," he saw the Sunday School movement as a threat to the work of the church that would ultimately lead Christians away from the truth of the gospel.

Not to be discouraged, the "pioneer nine," David Roper and eight other Sunday School members, banded together to create a new church named the Second Baptist Church. They immediately started strengthening their beloved Sunday School.

The Sunday School of the Second Baptist Church did not die, nor did the thousands of other Bible study organizations which have been started since that pivotal point, 1820, in the lives of Virginia Baptists. One reason the Sunday School movement did not vanish is because of godly laymen and laywomen, who recognized the power and potential of building units which would teach the Word of God and minister in the love of Jesus.

Southern Baptists have been greatly influenced by the leadership of the laity, especially in the examples of a young Mississippi businessman and a North Carolina farmer. One

One reason the Sunday School movement did not vanish is because godly laypersons recognized the power and potential of building units which would teach the Word of God and minister in the love of Jesus.

99

The Sunday School has been ably staffed by laypersons since its beginning more than two hundred years ago.

helped to create the "science of church growth," and the other led in an aggressive plan of evangelism, never experienced before or after his period of leadership.

One of those laymen was Arthur Flake, and the other was J. N. Barnette. The astonishing growth of the period of these two gentlemen's leadership greatly strengthened the churches and provided resources never known before. Coupled with the economical health of America, churches were able to move into new avenues of missions and ministry.

One of these expanded areas centered around personnel. Growing congregations were experiencing assimilation needs; and, with more people to serve, greater demands were placed on pastors. Soon new positions such as ministers of education, ministers of administration, and age-group ministers of all types were added to the ministerial staff. The work of the personnel committee brought new challenges as the paradigm of pastor, staff, and people was created. Certainly this step was needed, and the end results have been reassuring as ministerial staff and members have wrought great things in the name of the Lord.

One downside to this enlarged, professional, ministerial base has been the tendency for the "paid staff" suddenly to begin taking on the responsibility of "doing the work of ministry." After all, were not these people trained at the seminary, and were they not considered to be "pros"? Soon most of the visitation and decision making was vested in the hands of the professional minister.

Nowhere was this more prevalent

100

than in the Sunday School organization, which had been so ably staffed by laypersons for over 200 years. The addition of full-time staff continued to push the average lay leader more into the background. There was no conspiracy to the direction; but over a period of time, it became easier for everyone to say: "Let the minister of education do it. After all that is what we pay him to do, and he certainly has more time than I have. I have to do this task."

I encountered this trend early in my own ministerial career. I had been working on staff with a wonderful pastor who truly could be considered a "Sunday School man." He had always built the churches he served through the Sunday School organization.

One day he called me into his office and announced: "Bill, this is a 'cutting edge' church. We want to stay ahead in leadership, and I have decided that the old way of enlisting workers through the nominating committee is arcane and out of date. We have a fine ministerial staff who know more about this congregation than any layperson. I am going to cancel the work of the nominating committee, and from this time on the church staff will enlist all of the leaders."

That sounded good to me, and I immediately moved into the enlistment process, gladly bypassing the lay-led organization of the congregation. After all, I could make decisions faster; and I did not have to worry about a committee reaching consensus.

I thought the approach of using the abilities and controlled time of the professional staff members served me well in the art of build-

Laypersons desire to give themselves to significant ministry—like the Sunday School.

101

God gifts members of congregation to do the work of ministry He wants them to do.

ing growing Sunday Schools. In many ways this plan was successful for about 10 years. I was soon to learn, much to the dismay of my overall health and sanity, that this new filter of conducting enlistment was to reach obsolescence earlier than anyone expected.

The demands of the 80s and the incredible growth experienced in churches quickly moved the use of the staff member to being in charge of and conducting most of the business of the Sunday School into a precarious position. Just as the pastor had considered the nominating committee to be passé, the frustrations of the church staff in not being able to perform all of the duties expected brought a realization that something was wrong.

After several years of frenzied schedules and shouldering responsibilities too heavy for any one minister or any one staff, I finally realized that Paul was correct when he wrote about God's equipping the body for the work of ministry (see Eph. 4:12). God expects His work to be accomplished by His people in concert with His ministers. It is not to be attempted alone in either case.

The Sunday School organization and movement must be given back to the Robert Raikes of every generation—laypersons who love God and are "called according to His purposes" (Rom. 8:29, NASB).[1]

Twice a year Sunday School leaders from the various states come to the Sunday School Board for orientation and encouragement. They participate in strategic planning, review new products, provide feedback concerning resources and field service, and share needs

102

from their various states. The agenda is always packed; and, because the time is limited during their visits, the days are long and fatiguing.

During the meeting of May 1995, after a particularly stressful day, I awakened early in the morning, thinking about the presentation I would make to the state directors, challenging them to the great work which could be done. After my one, and only one, cup of coffee for the day, I went on-line with SBCNet to check the news of the day. The bulletin board had a flashing message for me, and I pulled it up on my computer screen. It was from a young man named Tommy Pophin. Here is the message I received from him at 5:00 a.m.:

Professional staff and lay leaders can work together to grow an excellent Sunday School.

Hi Bill,

I was wondering if you could answer a question for me. I just read excerpts from the Sunday School directors conference that you presented. I would like to know if you would share about how the minister of education and the Sunday School director work together. I am a minister of education, and I do not use a Sunday School director for the simple reason that anyone who even begins to look like an expert in Sunday School is put in as a department or division director. We cannot afford to have a Sunday School director. Can you give me some words that will convince me I am wrong? Thanks for your help.

Tommy

My immediate response in the early morning, after the tiring day before, was: "Oh, me, I don't have time for this answer. I will have to answer this when I feel more chipper. I am certainly not in the mood to try to convince any-

103

The Sunday School director is essential in leading the Sunday School to do the tasks it's assigned to do.

one about why he should use a Sunday School director."

I noticed that other messages were attached to Tommy's inquiry, and I started moving through each conversation. Suddenly, my eyes were riveted on an extended reply provided to Tommy's concern.

The entire email is included as I read it that morning:

Boy, is this a hot one! Until this time last year, I, too, served as Sunday School director for my church, since I believed that "we couldn't afford a director." When God really dealt with my heart, I realized that there is more to my responsibility than to direct a Sunday School. There was no way I could do it myself.

What does my Sunday School director do? How does he help me?

• He holds me accountable spiritually.

• He keeps the Sunday School focused and on target.

• He promotes outreach and caring ministries.

• He coordinates recruiting. He assists preschool, children, youth, and adult directors in their recruiting efforts.

• He encourages the creation of new units. He can do this better than I can, and I have the scars to prove it!

• He focuses on enlarging the organization. In September 1993, we went from two worship services and one Sunday School to three worship services and two Sunday Schools. In August of this year, we will move back to two worship services and two Sunday Schools (due to opening of new worship space). This is two complete reorganizations of our Sunday Schools in two years. The details were handled by our Sunday School director.

• He promotes training and development. He organizes our annual pilgrimages to Ridgecrest and handles

104

other training events.

In short, he does all the things you're probably doing at the expense of all the things you'd rather be doing! Yes, the secret's out. I have Superman as a Sunday School director. Not really, but I do have a godly man who is dedicated to the work of Sunday School. Is he a teacher of teachers? No! He is a leader of leaders! He motivates, he dreams, he plans, he implements, he encourages, and he builds the team.

So what's left for me to do during Sunday School?

• I roam the halls Sunday mornings and encourage all of our Sunday School leaders.

The Sunday School director is a leader of leaders.

• I participate in multiple worship services through preaching and prayer.

• I spend 10-15 minutes on Wednesday nights encouraging, motivating, and communicating to all our Sunday School leaders.

• I troubleshoot and provide resources where needed.

So what am I doing instead of Sunday School?

• Developing leaders who will develop other leaders.

• Building relationships with people who can build relationships with others.

• Trying to live out Philippians 4:8-9.

• Coordinating construction of a new building.

• Managing an office.

• Encouraging and motivating church leaders.

• Recruiting and training as requested.

• Encouraging VBS leaders.

• Starting support group ministries.

• Starting Promise Keepers and men's ministries.

• Starting women's ministries.

• Expanding weekday early education programs.

• Preparing for revival.

• Assisting deacons to reorganize care groups/family ministry.

I was a little dense, and it took too long to realize the

105

truth in the principle that unless I give my ministry away to others, I'm limiting kingdom work by my abilities. Find people who are teachable and willing, equip them and turn them loose!

When lay leaders and professional staff partner to do the work of the Sunday School, tasks are not duplicated. Rather more needs are met, more lives are saved, and more teachers are trained.

I could not believe what I was reading. Suddenly the fatigue of the prior day was gone, and my spirits were lifted. I reconsidered what I had always known as I had given my ministry in churches.

I had arisen to try to get ready to encourage others in a scheduled speech, but God had a message of hope and inspiration for me, provided by someone named Neal.

Ministers such as Neal Cordle, Tommy Pophin, and Bill Taylor will do well to involve laypeople in ministry.

Robert Raikes saw a need on the streets of Gloschester. Using his quick mind and able spirit, he directed all of his resources to making a difference in the lives of people. He is said to have remarked, "The world marches forward on the feet of little children." I think he understood the spirit of Christ who said, "Suffer the little children to come unto me, and forbid them not: for of such is the kingdom of God" (Mark 10:14).

Let's give the Sunday School back to Robert Raikes—a symbol of every layperson in the land.

Laypersons long to serve in effective ministry. What more effective ministry can they find than the Sunday School!

106

Personal Learning Activities

Consider the list of Sunday School director tasks and those of the minister of education in Neal Cordle's email message. How are similar tasks assigned in your church?

[1]From the *New American Standard Bible.* © The Lockman Foundation, 1960, 1962, 1963, 1968, 1971, 1972, 1973, 1975, 1977. Used by permission. Subsequent quotations marked NASB.

"Build relationships that build relationships."
—Neal Cordle

Chapter 12

The Employment Agency of the Church

"**G**od made you as you are in order to use you as he planned."

—S. C. McAuley

"The employment agency of the church. Wow! That is great, Bill. Where did you come up with that concept?" The person speaking was Linda Lawson, director of communications at the Sunday School Board. She had just read materials that would be used in *Facts and Trends* to explain directives concerning my new ministry as director of the Bible Teaching-Reaching Division.

I replied: "Arthur Flake wrote a book in 1930 called *The True Function of the Sunday School*. One of the chapters was entitled 'The Sunday School Is the Employment Agency of the Church.'"

Arthur Flake was always ahead of his time, but he was

We are like trees. We must create new leaves —new directions —in order to grow.

never more on target for the future than when he shared how to involve disciples in ministry. A close examination of the churches which have grown dramatically during the past 15 years, and also those which show promise of continuing this growth trend, reveals that they know how to employ or engage their members in meaningful ministry. To succeed, the churches of tomorrow will model the New Testament style of ministry more than the churches of the past 50 years.

I became a believer when I was 19 years old, not having a strong background of regular church attendance. One of the first things I noticed as a new church member was that most of the ministry was done by the pastor and the few staff members who assisted. If things were in order on Sundays and the ministry of hospital care and prospect visitation was completed by the "preacher," then everyone seemed to be satisfied.

It was a natural for one of the members to request that the preacher visit a family member or prospect to explain how one could become a Christian. After all, isn't that what the pastor is paid to do? And the pastor has been to seminary.

Two things are obvious about this pattern of ministry. The first is, it is totally ineffective.

During my seminary days, I had the privilege of serving with Howard Scott. He was pastor of Field Street Baptist Church in Cleburne, Texas; and he allowed me to serve in my first responsibility as minister of education. He was an able leader and had a great love for missions.

110

In a mentoring role, one day he said: "Bill, I have been the pastor of a church with 25 in attendance; today I pastor more than 2,200 members. I have never shepherded a congregation which was not too big for me. There is always one more visit or telephone call to make. The task God has given to us is so great that we dare not think we are ever qualified to do it without His help." He had learned, through his experience as a businessman prior to pastoral duties, that the church staff can never meet the demands of the congregation, not to mention the crush of the community.

The needs of society will not permit professional ministers to do the work of the church. Laity must do the work, or it will not be done.

The fact that many churches have experienced such a limited impact on society is an indication that an approach to Sunday School work or any other ministry area of the church will not work when laypersons are left out of the process. I wonder how many godly pastors literally had their hearts broken because they could not break this practice imposed on them by a well-meaning congregation.

The second problem with a pastor-staff-dominated ministry is that God's Word teaches that all members of the body are essential. Reading Ephesians 4:11-12 (NASB),[1] "And He gave some as apostles, and some as prophets, and some as evangelists, and some as pastors and teachers, for the equipping of the saints for the work of service, to the building up of the body of Christ," is enough to discard this old relic from the past. God never intended a group of professional ministers to carry out the Great Commission by themselves.

The needs of churches and communities will not permit this old paradigm of min-

111

The churches of tomorrow will model the New Testament style of ministry more than the churches of the last 50 years.

istry. There is simply too much to do for a selected group to be able to accomplish everything that is possible in such an arena.

The fall of 1982 was one of the most difficult periods in my life. The previous three and one half years had been spent in the delightful atmosphere of University Baptist Church in Coral Gables, Florida. The spirit was one of excitement; the people were loving and thoughtful; and I had the greatest respect for the pastor, Dan Yeary.

In the midst of my happiness, my immediate family went through a difficult time. Miami of the early eighties was a city in turmoil, and the crime and tension of the city pressed on my family. Engaged in the turmoil of the city because of the hurts of church members and friends, we were also dealing with the possibility of a move as I began to feel God's call to ministry in another location.

My youngest son, Brent, was about 11 years old; and my older son, Billy, was a senior in high school. We had a family practice of assigning one of the four family members to be the "preacher for the week" at our devotional period. I am still amused when I think of times Brent provided leadership and wanted to break the family unit into "small groups." The sharing times made apparent the stress we were feeling.

During one devotional, I promised my three significant others that if they would pray about staying in Miami I would pray about being open to a new work. I have said that I kept my part of the agreement; I was never sure they did!

In time I felt that God was definitely leading me to accept the position of minister of

112

education and administration at the newly formed Prestonwood Baptist Church in developing North Dallas. I had never seen a church in such a whirlwind. As B. C. Brown of Zeigler Bond Company said, "This was a church on a roll."

More than two hundred prospects visited each week. As many as 50 people joined the church on Sunday—35 of whom we often had never seen before. Nobody but the pastor even had an office. Most staff ministers did not have any support staff assistance. During the first nine months, I graded the entire Sunday School twice because of the rapid growth.

The church was using a computer service, but at that time only two lists were available—E and L, early and late Sunday Schools. If you wanted information to analyze what was happening to the people, you received 1,500 on each sort.

Between November 1982 and February 1983, a small task force led by a volunteer I enlisted made more than 20,000 corrections on a membership list of 3,000 names. These corrections included zip codes, telephone numbers, and class assignments. Before that time it was almost impossible to do anything because of the inconsistency of the record system.

On top of that confusion, the church had overspent its income by $200,000. One of my first assignments was to mount an aggressive stewardship program to make sure this did not happen again.

I did a foolish thing during these frantic days. I did not take a full day off from work in almost three and one half months. I

Success often depends on a leader's ability to share the work load.

113

"And He gave some as apostles, and some as prophets, and some as evangelists, and some as pastors and teachers, for the equipping of the saints for the work of service, to the building up of the body of Christ."
—Ephesians 4:11-12 (NASB)

became sick physically and emotionally.

We were preparing to enter the new worship center shortly after the first of 1983, and I was so fatigued I could hardly place one foot in front of the other. I had come to the end of my resources. In fact, I experienced down days during that period directly related to fatigue. One thing I learned out of this experience is that when people tell me that they are depressed I do not take their statements lightly. I knew I was not functioning well, but I could not break the cycle.

One day I got on my knees and simply asked God to help me. These were not well-rehearsed platitudes but rather a desperate cry that I could not go on. I feared failing my family. I felt that my peers viewed me as a failure. I knew that this fine group of caring people deserved better than what I had to give.

Out of those hours of deep introspection, I felt led to start meeting with the people of the church. I shared important assignments which were critical to the success of strategic ministries at Prestonwood. I emphasized that I wanted their affirmative response only if they felt deeply in their souls that this was exactly what God would have them to do. These were not small jobs but rather those which would impact not only Prestonwood Baptist Church but also people throughout the world. These tasks could not be taken lightly.

Eureka! I found that the people not only would, not only could; but when they accepted these major responsibilities in the name of the Lord, they could also do it so much better than any minister in sight. The jobs were

114

completed in fine fashion, but much more important was the fact that when the people were given an opportunity to serve they bought into the process.

The members who served on the Saturday Nights in Dallas Concert Ministry Team are prime examples of people in service. This once-a-month concert series required a myriad of tasks to get the job done. Tickets were sold in Christian bookstores. Artists were transported back and forth from the airport. Stage sets were built, and lights were positioned for the programs. People were needed to assist in parking cars and distributing programs. Even those who cleaned up the auditorium after the concerts were finished on Saturday night are typical of what happened in the hearts of the volunteers.

The next Sunday morning all Saturday Nights in Dallas helpers were in Sunday School, studying God's Word. Since they had a part, they were as interested in what was going on in the life of the church as the pastor. The joy the members experienced from performing their own God-led ministry encouraged responsible membership. They became active participants in ministry rather than supportive spectators who absented themselves at the slightest provocation.

Growing churches provide significant ministry for their members. All Christians need to discover service which they consider to be uniquely assigned to them by the Spirit of God.

During the first days of new member orientation, I always told new members the following:

Laypersons, as well as professional staff ministers, perform best when the task is significant, they feel called to the work, and they are accountable and affirmed for what they do.

115

Growing churches provide significant ministry for their members.

• Seek God's leadership in your participation.

• Do not accept any responsibility unless you feel led of the Holy Spirit.

• If you find yourself serving in a role in which you are uncomfortable about the rightness of the task for you, go to the person who enlisted you and share your convictions about the matter. (I have discovered that laypersons often are reticent about this step, especially if the enlister is the pastor, a staff member, or a lay leader who is personally significant to them. They fear being branded as one who is not supportive or cannot be trusted to do a job.)

• Be selective about how many responsibilities you accept.

• Serve with excellence in all that you do accept.

The Sunday School, or Bible Teaching-Reaching Ministry of a church, does not have enough jobs to offer opportunities for service for all members. This realization becomes an advantage because it immediately places Sunday School leaders in a partnering role with every other ministry in the church. Because ministries are limitless, often going without enough people to do the job well, the astute Bible study leader will actively assist all avenues of ministry in the congregation. This visible encouragement reinforces the importance of the Bible Teaching-Reaching organization.

Recent years have brought forth a new phrase, "Give the ministry away." This represents the biblical pattern of participation.

Howard Scott was right. The small church is too big for you and me. The medium-size congregation overwhelms you and me. The

116

megachurch is impossible for you and me.

The task is too big. We certainly cannot do the work in our own strength. As Jesus lovingly taught His closest followers, "Without me, you can do nothing" (see John 15:5). But regardless of church size, ministry is never too large for the body of believers. God's Word has a deliberate plan which involves every member of the congregation in meaningful service and ministry—a plan which stimulates personal growth in the Lord.

The Bible Teaching-Reaching Ministry—the Sunday School—is truly the employment agency of the church.

Laypersons who get involved in the work of the church become active participants in ministry rather than supportive spectators.

Personal Learning Activities

1. How is the Sunday School the employment agency of the church? How does this concept apply to other areas of church ministry and work?

2. Why is it not good for the pastor and staff ministers to do all the work of the church?

3. What are the benefits of lay involvement?

[1]From the *New American Standard Bible.* © The Lockman Foundation, 1960, 1962, 1963, 1968, 1971, 1972, 1973, 1975, 1977. Used by permission. Subsequent quotations marked NASB.

Chapter 13
Weathering Storms

"We are healed of a suffering only by experiencing it to the full."

—**Marcel Proust**[1]

One of the greatest promises given to the believer by the Lord is, "I am with you always until the end of the world" (see Matt. 28:20). All Christians face times in ministry when they feel they have come to the end of the world.

If this has not already happened to you, it will. No matter who you are or how well you are doing, events will transpire which will upset everything in your world. Your devastating event may come out of the blue, and you may have had nothing to do with the event, but you are affected. Or you may have made choices which cause you distress. Either way, you have the opportunity to understand how much encouragement can be received from the only One who sees and understands all aspects of the situation.

Church Politics

When I first started my work in education, I served a congregation which was unhappy with its pastor. Well-meaning members

119

took actions which ultimately caused great distress in the fellowship. Finally, an occasion came when someone had to take a stand against what they were doing behind the scenes. When I gained the courage to face these people, other members were inspired to join the cause; and as a result of their involvement, the church returned to a productive course. I learned that we must not be afraid of what people can do, but we must follow the directions of the One who first called us.

"Lo, I am with you."

Educational Procedures

I do not believe you can build a lasting Sunday School organization without leader preparation. At the beginning of a church year, after plans are drawn and their execution begun, leaders swiftly discover that not every teacher sees the importance of intense preparation. In fact, many will say outright, "When the division director asked me to teach, she never told me I had to attend weekly workers meeting; and I do not plan to attend."

After a Sunday School revival with the Sunday School pioneer, Leon Kilbreth, I decided that we could not continue to allow our Sunday School to be crippled because we did not pay the price in preparation to be the best we could possibly be. This meant that a greater effort would be placed on attending the weekly faculty preparation meeting. Our leaders taught every week, and they needed to prepare every week. This was a worthy thought but an action which brought many sleepless nights.

One teacher marshalled her entire class to thwart my efforts to build a strong, func-

120

tioning Sunday School. After my office was inundated with calls from members who were disturbed that I would ask the teachers to attend this training meeting, I wondered if it was worth the aggravation.

One afternoon on my way home from a tiring day, I was literally overcome by a sense of God's Spirit in my life. I pulled to the side of the road and thanked the Lord for the privilege of being in the fray. I realized that what the leadership of the church was attempting to do was good and would ultimately richly bless the existing members and those who would be reached in the days ahead. The prize was worth the stormy trip.

Teachers teach weekly, and they should prepare weekly.

Human Frailties

September 21, 1988, was an eventful day for me and the entire membership at Prestonwood Baptist Church. The church was involved in an incredible effort to start a fully graded Sunday School and worship service on Saturday nights.

Gigantic plans had been executed in a relatively brief period. Trips had been made to Willow Creek Community Church near Chicago to investigate what was being done through this creative congregation. Our church leaders had enlisted more than a thousand members who pledged to move their worship and Bible study time to Saturday nights. Their commitment would allow the church to continue growing at a rate previously unheard of in any Southern Baptist church.

In the midst of this excitement, a credible member came to me on the third floor

121

"These are times in which a genius would wish to live. It is not in the still calm of life, or in the repose of a pacific station, that great characters are formed. Great necessities call out great virtues."
—Abigail Adams[2]

of the Christian learning center and informed me that our pastor would be leaving the church under difficult circumstances.

My world suddenly stopped. How could this be?

Three days later the new Saturday schedule was kicked off with 2,200 in worship and more than 1,000 in Bible study groups. Everyone was ecstatic, but no one knew what I was thinking as I watched the local NBC affiliate covering Prestonwood, saying the church was on the "cutting edge of reaching people" and this new concept in programs was another living example of what could be done when baby boomers were provided choices.

During the two weeks prior to the pastor's resignation, the world continued to close in on me. I went from sadness concerning the tragedy to anger. All the hours of hard work were being jeopardized. The ministers on the staff began meeting daily to pray together.

I will always remember the horrifying feelings I experienced on that fateful Saturday when the *Dallas Morning News* carried the story about the resignation of the pastor of Prestonwood Baptist Church. I felt as if I were reading about somebody else in another church in another place. A few hours later that same morning, I knew it was not distant as I listened to my pastor of six years read his resignation.

The first Sunday after the resignation was difficult, with people experiencing shock and grief over the lost leadership of one they deeply admired and appreciated. A newsperson came to me to ask what position the church would take concerning the resignation of the

122

founding pastor. That same night, I tried to give the answer to the question by saying that the position Prestonwood would take would be before the Lord. I called on the members to fast and pray. Churchwide prayer meetings were scheduled at 6:00 a.m. I remember the first morning I drove in sight of the church campus to see our prayer warriors ready to take their place on their knees before the Lord.

The next seven months were filled with moments just as dreadful and sorrowful; but, ultimately, I could see God's hand on this wonderful congregation when a pastor search committee of 18 people brought a unanimous recommendation concerning a new pastor. Over two thousand members, voting by secret ballot, affirmed the work of the committee and thanked the Lord for His healing process.

God is at work in the midst of our adversities.

People fail, and all will ultimately disappoint, but God is good. He truly is "an ever present help in time of trouble" (see Ps. 46:1).

I have often said that one of the greatest joys I have ever experienced has been the privilege of working with pastors. One godly leader, with whom I worked during the early part of my ministry was Hubert Christian. He had completed only one year of college, but I do not think I have ever met anyone who has studied the Word of God any more intensely than he had. He shared some fatherly advice with me on one occasion. "Bill, when the Lord starts moving dramatically in your ministry and you start 'kicking the devil,' be ready because the devil will start kicking you."

This man, without a degree of any kind, who had learned from the Holy Spirit,

123

We serve a Master who can speak a word and cause a turbulent moment to flow into a peaceful calm

taught me a wonderful lesson. He prepared me for the storms which would ultimately come in my work. He could not forecast what these storms might be, but he helped me prepare for their onslaught.

Just as faithful believers have walked through difficult times, so will the Christian educator of the 21st century. Storms of any generation cause fear and discomfort, but we serve a Master who can speak a word and cause a turbulent moment to flow into a peaceful calm. As moved as I am by that truth, I am more encouraged by the fact that if the Lord chooses not to quieten the winds of sorrow, He will be an "ever present help as we walk through the tempest" (see Ps. 46:1).

Personal Learning Activities

1. What storms has your church faced? Did they come at a time of growth? How did church leaders respond?

2. What personal storms have you weathered? In what ways were you aware of God's presence?

[1]Marcel Proust (1871-1922), *The Sweet Cheat Gone*, 165.
[2]Abigail Adams (1744-1818), in a letter to John Quincy Adams, 19 Jan. 1780.

124

Chapter 14

Blessings of Mentoring

"A community is like a ship; every one ought to be prepared to take the helm."

—Henrik Ibsen[1]

The Bible Teaching-Reaching Division of the Sunday School Board has the privilege of working with 39 state Sunday School groups. Traditionally, their leaders attend two annual meetings where the personnel from the states and the Bible Teaching-Reaching Division meet together to evaluate the work of the past and plan for the future. During the May 1995 meeting, we had experienced a long, arduous day of study; and because of the extended meeting periods, I received just a few hours of rest before starting the next day.

In chapter 11, "Give Sunday School Back to Robert Raikes," I related how I check SBCNet and my CompuServe number to see if I have email messages. When I opened up the SBCNet connection, I was greeted with the message concerning the Sunday School director. I shared that email message in my next presentation.

As soon as I finished the presentation, every state director wanted a personal copy of the message; and I promised that I would send it to them immediately. In fact, the message was sent to their

125

Technology offers new ways to develop mentoring relationships.

offices, via SBCNet, almost before they could get checked out of their hotels at the end of the meeting.

As I investigated it further, the story continued with a different twist. I sent a word of encouragement to Neal Cordle, expressing my gratitude for his wisdom and example. Then I asked, "Who are you, and where do you minister?" I was not prepared for his reply; but seeing how the Lord works in our lives (as experienced by the relationship I have with Jim Neyland, as described in chapter 2), I should not have been surprised.

This was my message to Neal:

Neal, I want you to know that God has used you to bless the hearts of the entire BTR staff and 39 state Sunday School directors. The directors were so thrilled with your writings that they have requested a personal copy. Whoever you are, Neal, thank you for blessing our meeting today.

To my surprise, I received the following message the next day.

Bill,
Thanks for your kind words. I am blessed to serve Burnt Hickory Baptist Church in Marietta, Georgia, in the infamous Noonday Association. You and I have met a couple of times in passing—at Roswell Street during our conference two years ago and last summer at Ridgecrest.

I was a member of Northpointe Church—where Margaret Slusher's husband, Steve, is pastor—when God called me from an engineering position to vocational ministry. In 1989, we packed up for SWBTS. I

126

graduated in 1991 and came back to Marietta and continued my education as a charter member of our associational leadership team.

I have been in Tommy's shoes. He described my experience at my first church after seminary. About one and a half years ago, God moved us to Burnt Hickory. I spent the first six months in the same rut—falling all over a Sunday School director who knows his job. God dealt with me and changed my focus to equipping and empowering rather than gathering and smothering. My, how liberating!

We are in West Cobb County. East Cobb is full, so the people are coming here. We are growing rapidly and paddling furiously to keep up. A major portion of our success is the dedication of our lay leaders. We are just trying to stay out of God's way and let Him move and work.

Forming new relationships, using new technology, strengthens the work of the church.

Bill, I have prayed for you regularly since your move to the Board. I am excited about the possibilities of your vision. You have inspired me to get on the cutting edge. In fact, after Fast Track at Ridgecrest last summer, I took the plunge, bought a new laptop, and began using multimedia in my presentations. You encouraged me and enabled me to be a better leader and teacher by stretching my imagination.

One of the guys in the Bible Teaching-Reaching Division (who shall remain anonymous!) described you when you came to the Sunday School Board as one who "kicks up a lot of dust when he walks through." Some of that dust settled on me. Thank you, and may God continue to bless the Bible Teaching-Reaching Division.

Neal Cordle

Later I received another message from the person who had started the dialogue:

127

Personal relationships continue to be paramount in a high-tech world.

Bill:

I appreciate all of the input I have received from you and Neal. I am really going to make this a priority and a matter of prayer. One of the reasons I do not have a Sunday School director is because of a present shortage of leadership in our church. We are starting one to two new units in Sunday School every quarter. So I keep putting my leaders into those positions. Maybe it is time to find a leader for the Sunday School. You have been helpful. I appreciate your leadership. God bless your work.

Tommy Pophin

This chapter is a picture of ministry in the 21st century. The use of technology will bless scores of church leaders and individual congregations. What would have probably taken a year to share in earlier times was completed in a two-day period and distributed across America.

Don't miss the greatest truth of this chapter. Yes, computers are important for presentations and quick communications; but the key ingredient in this story is the personal relationships which were established in the past and will continue to reap harvest in the future.

I did not know that I had the privilege of "stirring up the dust" for a young man named Neal Cordle any more than J. N. Barnette knew that the truths of his cultivation and harvest would bless the generation which plowed after him.

One of the greatest blessings you will experience in the next century will be to help others prepare to take the helm of the ship.

128

Personal Learning Activities

1. How has technology enhanced the ministry of your church?

2. Who has mentored you without ever knowing it—from a book, a conference, a sermon? Perhaps this would be a good time to let them know.

[1]Henrik Ibsen (1828-1906), *An Enemy of the People*, Act 1.

The use of technology will bless scores of church leaders and individual congregations.

129

Chapter 15

Church Growth Explained by Those Who Have Never Experienced It

"**S**triving for success without hard work is like trying to harvest where you have not planted."

—David Bly

I am always amazed at how many people pass themselves off as church growth experts who have had little or no experience with church growth. They take surveys or visit growing churches and then go on the road, explaining the principles of church growth. After so many tellings and surveys, people begin to believe these consultants must know something about growing churches. Even though America has plenty of "experts," we still seem to have few growing churches.

When someone talks about how to build growing church-

A clear danger in today's society is to be moved or motivated by challenges which have not been challenged.

es, I always want to ask: "How did you do it? How did you overcome this barrier or that obstacle? Were there moments when you seemed to hit the wall and despite your most gallant effort you were unable to achieve success?"

Joe Hight is a dear friend. I met Joe soon after he retired as president of Dunn and Bradstreet. Officed in New York City, Joe provided leadership to one of America's premier companies and, because of his record of achievement, was considered a genius of finance in the United States. In his retirement he continues to serve his church and also to serve on several boards of Fortune 500 companies.

One day I asked Joe the following question, "Joe, when you attend an important meeting of the board of directors for a major company, how do you know when the vast amount of data provided is not used as a camouflage to keep you from knowing the true condition of the organization?"

His reply was crisp and precise. "Bill, if anyone tries to put something over on the board, or if they do not know what they are talking about, I can have them climbing the walls in less than five minutes."

I was impressed. This brilliant man, who had dedicated his life in fiscal matters, was prepared to meet any challenge in this arena.

Then I thought, *I can do the same thing in the realm of ministry.*

I have the privilege of visiting various churches or leading conferences from time to time. I have learned that it is relatively easy to walk into a church some distance away and exhort them to "get with it." After about 30 min-

132

utes on the field, I see various characteristics that are easily recognized, and I also know where to find the hot spots—those areas which are naturally difficult to build such as workers planning meetings, especially weekly ones. After querying the leaders about their shortcomings, the rest is easy. I exhort the people that they must correct their weaknesses if they are to function effectively.

Of course, these hot spots, such as workers planning meetings, are important; but the fact is they are often difficult to implement. Making them work on an ongoing basis is even harder. Everybody is for them, but few are able to execute them. My point is that it is one thing to observe that they should be done but another to actually do them. I want to listen to those who have been instrumental in building effective models.

Only champions can adequately call the game.

It is time to champion the builders, not the observers. Let's hear from those who have not only dreamed but also who have achieved. They are the ones who started the race and also finished it. They are the ones who have something to say. They certainly are knowledgeable concerning the intricate parts which are critical for success.

Church builders are usually understanding because they know what a great price must be paid and how many trying times a church encounters on the way to victory. They also realize that many times they have had little to do with the end results. The Lord just chose to work in a special manner. They continue to work during the gray days as well as the bright ones.

133

Those who have finished the race have something to say.

A clear danger in today's society is to be moved or motivated by challenges which have not been challenged. Too many things are being said which must not be allowed to be considered fact without scrutiny. This close examination is not for the sake of causing embarrassment, nor does it mean the challenges are untrue. Rather, if it has value, that value is enhanced by investigation which augments its findings.

During the summer of 1995, Dick Lincoln, pastor of Shandon Baptist Church in Columbia, South Carolina, made the following comment to the participants at a Sunday School Training Conference at Glorieta, New Mexico. He said, "A half-truth can become a whole lie."

As I listened to his sermon, my thoughts jumped immediately to a speaker who had visited the church I served in Dallas. A claim made during the presentation at a church growth conference quickly was reduced by almost 50 percent when a few questions were privately asked concerning the results. The speaker was not prevaricating about the accomplishments; he was simply not clearly qualifying the statement.

Recently I engaged Rick Warren in a conversation about a movement in the church growth discipline. Rick serves as the founding pastor of the Saddleback Community Church in Mission Viejo, California. He brings much credibility to his observations because of his record of accomplishments. Almost animated, Rick stated: "This sounds good, and it reads well in books. The only problem is, it just doesn't work in the churches." I walked away from the conversation

134

with Rick, thinking about how many leaders would be less than enthusiastic about this unproved approach in ministry if they had only been privileged to have heard from this practitioner.

I am reminded that many excellent teachers are able to teach certain disciplines which they have not actually commanded. Some of the better coaches have never been great athletes themselves, but they have instructed students who were able to achieve goals which the coaches could only dream about.

I also fear that the tone of this chapter might sound harsh and all-knowing. That certainly is not my intent.

But I remain convinced that certain things in life are best understood by those who have experienced firsthand the joys and trials of the endeavor. What may appear to be relatively simple may actually be complex, and what seems to be overwhelming may be disguised from its simplicity.

The New York Times News Service carried an article in a recent publication concerning the use of analysts for professional tennis matches. A debate had taken place concerning whether a student of the game could provide as much insight as one who had been on the courts. The tennis professional contended that "only champions can adequately call top-level tennis." He said: "You feel you're in a select group. You're number one. You know strategies and have been in that position hundreds of times more than others."[1]

The disciples asked Jesus to teach them to pray not because of what He had said

Church growth ideas may sound good, but those that have been tested and adapted to meet particular needs are more likely to yield results.

135

The disciples asked Jesus to teach them to pray—not because of what He said about prayer but because they saw Him praying.

about prayer but because they saw the most effective model, the Master praying.

When one has been blessed to be instrumental in church growth, he or she has something valid to share. Those blessed to have experienced church growth must realize that the Lord gave them everything; they are not to become puffed up. Those who make inquiry need to understand that they are also sharing with another "pilgrim" who is to be respected but not reverenced.

Personal Learning Activities

1. Do you, as a leader, try what others have tried, try what you have read about, or try to adapt both to meet the needs of your people under the leadership of the Holy Spirit?

2. What can church leaders learn from an admonition to test the validity of those who tell them how to grow a church?

[1]"Mac Puts His Money Where His Mouth Is," 2 September 1995.

Chapter 16
Be Careful What You Call Innovative

"**W**herever you see a successful enterprise, someone once made a courageous decision."

—**Peter Drucker**

Our culture and vocabulary are interesting. Trends and words take on a new life, changing in meaning and acceptance over time. A casual observation concerning interrelationships between generations gives a hint of this phenomenon when either the older or younger generation shares a practice of their particular culture or one of their buzzwords. Eyebrows may rise on the older crowd, and uplifted eyes of the younger people may signal a completely different interpretation of what is valued or said. No generation has ever been spared this exercise, and one marvels as to the rapidity of one's movement from one group to another.

What young person understands "Over There . . . Over There," and what older generation would have ever related to "Not!" or "You can't touch that!"

One phrase which has been used during the last 15 years

The term *small group* is used to signify the importance of relationship and caring in our society today.

in the realm of church growth has been *small groups.* It is used to signify the importance of relationships and caring in our society and has taken on new life in Bible study groupings. It is a wonderful use of the term; and in this world of tension and stress, it is a means to balancing high tech with high touch.

I have to confess that at times this proves somewhat aggravating to me when people forget that Southern Baptists promoted "small group" ministry in the Sunday School training sessions of B. W. Spilman and Arthur Flake long before most of today's church growth leaders were born.

The word *innovation* has come to have a new meaning in the life of the church today. When a church wants to make known that they are involved in a new way of doing things or accomplishing ministry, many times they classify this approach as innovative, a new paradigm.

Recently, I listened to a group of prominent Southern Baptist educators, meeting in Nashville, discuss church growth in their communities. As the conversation wore on, a recurring phrase dominated their conversations. When describing the new churches being started in their various locations, often they remarked, "In our state we have a blending of 'innovative churches' and more 'traditional models.'"

I did not pay particular attention to this terminology at first; but when it kept coming back into the discussions, my attention was pricked each time the word *innovation* was used. Much of the ministry in which I have been privileged to participate has been classified by

138

Southern Baptists and other church-growth leaders as innovative in spirit and accomplishments. The word has never before taken on a total meaning, devoid of results.

Immediately, I remembered a conversation I had with a leader in a congregation in which I had served as a minister of education. I was seeking to practice two of the key points of the Flake Formula, starting new classes and enlisting workers. Because this person seemed threatened by this approach, which meant that much work would have to be done to make these two principles work, he challenged me with the following statement, "Bill, would you rather have one good teacher or four weak teachers?"

My reply was: "That is not much of a choice. Sure, I would rather have one good teacher than four who cannot do the job; but I would rather do the work of preparation, training, and motivation and have the possibility of four excellent teachers—four excellent teachers who will reproduce themselves over time, giving me eight excellent teachers, who will ultimately follow this pattern, enabling our church to have a teaching, ministering army of Bible teachers, who will shake our community and the world for Christ. Now, that is the choice I want and a choice which I am prepared to pay for in sacrifice and determination."

The manner in which I heard these Christian educators speaking left me with another "lose-lose choice." I want to be with the innovative crowd. Why would I even think of being labeled as "old," "ineffective," "dated," or "not relevant"?

Small-group ministry in Southern Baptist churches is not new. It is called "Sunday School."

139

Innovative has come to mean "new paradigm."

Don't use the term *innovative* with me unless you are referring to a means of seeing the Great Commission carried out as never before in the history of Christianity. A work cannot be described as innovative if form is the only criteria for evaluation.

One does not have an innovative ministry because:

• An electrical instrument is played instead of an organ and Scripture choruses are sung to the neglect of hymns.

• Worship is scheduled on a day other than Sunday morning.

• Bible study is not provided along with worship on Sunday mornings.

• Bible study units are called "small groups" instead of Sunday School.

• Members dress casually at all church events.

• A new vocabulary is regularly used, such as "user friendly."

• Business terms and practices are transferred to the church environment.

• A departure is made from the system currently in vogue.

I have been a believer and a Southern Baptist for 37 years. I admire most of what Southern Baptists have stood for during their history, especially related to believing and practicing the truths of the Word of God and their emphasis on world evangelism and world missions.

One trait of my denomination that I have never understood is their tendency to start something new at the expense of whatever is happening. It seems that often, in order to sell the valuable points of a new approach or a new

140

product, it can only be done by undermining the old approach or describing in great detail the shortcomings of the material currently used.

This happened with the organization of membership training, once called Training Union or Church Training and now called Discipleship Training. When I was a new Christian, I often heard conference leaders or speakers make disparaging remarks such as the fact that "Training Union members read portions of the study materials, often called 'parts,' to one another during their sessions on Sunday evenings." It did not take long for these barbs of criticism to take their toll, and a once-strong training opportunity started a downward trend. Perhaps many of the observations were correct, and adjustments needed to take place. My point is that few solutions were offered, especially those which had prototypes or had been proven. The end result was faster decline because of the lack of trust by everyone, including those who had faithfully participated in the learning opportunity and had benefited greatly from it.

It was many years before a new approach in membership training (such as MasterLife, *PrayerLife*, and *Experiencing God*) was accepted by church members; and the important task of "making disciples" was severely penalized during that interim—probably to a degree which could never be fully measured. I have often reflected, *The deacons and leaders who shared a role in those Sunday night programs knew a lot more about doctrines, church polity, and world missions than most Baptists I encounter today.*

My entire ministry has been associat-

Traditional is being used to imply "ineffective," "outdated," or "not relevant."

141

If Southern Baptists do not move aggressively back into the realm of unexplored possibilities, our brightest days will be viewed as in the past.

ed with pastors and churches who were considered by many to be on the cutting edge of innovative ministries. When one referred to some endeavor or missions outreach as being effective in reaching people, we always experienced joy because the Lord had allowed us to be a part of a creative opportunity.

My quarrel is not with innovation. In fact, I personally believe that if Southern Baptists do not move aggressively back into the realm of unexplored possibilities, our brightest days will be viewed as in the past. I do not want *innovative* to be used in such a way that it implies a wrong standard or denigrates a successful tool.

A church or an individual is innovative when:

• People are being reached with the good news of Jesus Christ.

• Effective ministry, both in outreach and in maturation, is occurring.

• Potential leaders are being enlisted, equipped, and placed into service.

• Current leaders are growing spiritually.

• The entire membership is continually moving toward Christlikeness.

• God is given the glory for everything that happens.

• There is an openness to what God is already doing.

• The message takes priority over the method.

The business community uses terms such as *R&D* (research and development) and *cash cow* (core business). Normally, about 15 to 20 percent of a company's income will be provided for research and development to make

142

sure the company continually improves and does not lose market share because the business environment changes. But, even though it places importance on this part of the system, it would never do anything to undermine, in the eyes of the customers or employees, the continued value of what has made the company what it is today and what it is doing to make everything possible, including research and development, in the future.

We, too, must exercise the same wisdom in our dealings with churches and church leaders. Our vocabulary can betray us. Why would we want to imply that ongoing, core work, Bible study—Sunday School, is limited, weak, or unfit for the days ahead.

When we use terms that pit one approach against another, we make a grave mistake. Even the usage of such terminology as *innovative churches versus traditional churches* weakens both. Who is to say that a church using processes with a proven history among Southern Baptists cannot be considered an innovative congregation. In fact, more churches that would be labeled "traditional" probably have a greater record of true innovation than any of the newer models.

The new work, which is classified as an "innovative church," is often not allowed time to prove the newer system actually works. It was interesting that many of the educators I heard in the meeting mentioned earlier felt that the majority of these trendy units seemed to plateau at an earlier stage than the traditional. We must allow time for maturation.

The Home Mission Board recently

A church is innovative when people are being reached with the good news of Jesus Christ.

143

A church is innovative when Christians are growing spiritually.

released information concerning the creation of new churches. The new starts, which tried the new approach, known as the "innovative churches," had a success rate of about one out of every 30 to 50 starts, while the traditional approach was running about one in every three.

Since the success rate of starting new churches with traditional methods is so much higher than the new models, does this mean the traditional is preferable for the future and has more potential because the failure rate is less? I don't think so. Could it be possible that the emerging paradigm will offer more in the future, thereby ensuring a brighter opportunity to reach people in an increasingly secular society? What a devastating decision it would be if the societal structure of the 21st century is geared toward this model and Christian educators missed it because of its poor percentage in successful church planting.

The business community understands that new products or services often need time, additional research, and trial and error before they arrive at the eureka moment that changes all dimensions and perspectives. History is filled with those who completed one more test or gave a project just a little more time to work out the deficiencies.

My experience has allowed me to be a part of many models of ministry, especially the tried-and-proven Sunday School and the small-group ministry. I have been privileged to hear the inner working systems of several approaches, including the Korean model used by the world's largest church.

144

I took several trips during the 80s to witness how such large numbers of people could be reached. For those who had never known a church much larger than 200 in attendance, just to imagine a church that claimed 50,000 members was astounding and then to see that congregation continue its rapid growth with a membership exceeding 600,000 today. Yet, in spite of the enthusiasm and the dreams of building a similar work in American churches, not many models have succeeded.

My questions are:

• Have we really understood the cultures where these models have flourished?

Sunday School is the "core work" of the church.

• Is there something about the mind-set of Americans that prohibits such a structure's ever being accepted?

• Or does the process just require time for adjustments and bringing the people along, carefully leading them to accept this new way?

Personally, even though I am a basic Sunday School person through and through, I really believe that the possibility and potential exists for the church of the living Lord to reach so many people with the gospel in the third millennium A.D. that a better, more effective process must be developed.

Let us not lose the opportunity by:

• Rushing the process. Be patient, let it find its way.

• Making claims for the new paradigm which it is not prepared to deliver at the moment.

• Undermining the present organization, the Sunday School, which has served believers so well in the past and still has a vital contribution to make in the future. The resources that will

145

Sunday School has served believers well in the past and will make a vital contribution in the future.

enable a search for new methods will come from the core ministry.

• Believing that the various approaches are really enemies.

If there is a better way to be effective in sharing the Great Commission with this generation, let us be first in line to embrace such a proposal. The Bible teaches that we are to honor our parents and those who are aged. That same honor can be encouraged as we allow strategies to develop which maximize the gifts of both the tried and proven and the "new kid on the block," which has the potential to keep our witness for the Lord strong and consistent, regardless of the age.

Personal Learning Activities

1. Most churches have characteristics that could be labeled innovative and characteristics that could be labeled traditional. Which characteristics, programs, or activities in your church would you label traditional? Which are innovative? Make a list. Which seem to be more effective?

2. Add to your list of innovative approaches those you know other churches in your area are doing. Check the list of criteria for innovations in this chapter. Do the approaches on your list measure up to these standards?

146

Chapter 17

Building a System That Works

"The real winners in life are the people who look at every situation with an expectation that they can make it work or make it better."

—Barbara Pletcher

A few years ago I served on the faculty of Sunday School Week at Ridgecrest Conference Center in North Carolina. The theme that week was "Coaching a Winning Sunday School." Various sessions were built around terminology found on the football field—blocking, passing, running, scouting, and staying eligible for the draft. The conference even included cheerleaders and concession vendors, reenacting the spirit of winning football enthusiasm as all participants were challenged to victory.

On my flight back to Dallas after the conference, I wondered, *Why are there so few winning Sunday School teams today?* I was pressed even harder to recall coaches (religious educators) who clearly fit the description of a winner.

Was it because no one has articulated what is to be done in building a winning Sunday School? Everyone knows there are basic football plays; you have to run, pass, block, and tackle. The one who has the highest score at the end of the game wins.

147

Flake Formula of
Sunday School
growth:
1. Know the
possibilities.
2. Enlist, train, and
motivate workers.
3. Enlarge the
organization.
4. Provide space.
5. Visit in the name
of the Lord.

Can we identify similar guidelines to building a winning Sunday School? We could list an infinite number of approaches to building an effective Bible study organization, but most Southern Baptists are familiar with the steps of the Flake Formula of Sunday School growth:

- Know the possibilities.
- Enlist, train, and motivate workers.
- Enlarge the organization.
- Provide space.
- Visit in the name of the Lord.

Most religious educators would say they believe and understand Flake's Formula. I can hardly remember a conference when some form of this formula has not been presented and affirmed. If so, why do we not have growing Sunday Schools everywhere?

Is it because of untrained leaders in the coaching ranks?—No, the church arena is blessed with the brightest, most articulate leaders ever. They have access to excellent training on all levels from universities and seminaries to local and national seminars, denominationally sponsored events, and new church growth conferences available at increasing offerings.

More ministers serve today with degrees past the bachelor's level than ever. These ministers not only have been thoroughly equipped for ministry, but also the opportunities for continued education are staggering—computer networks back into the seminary and denominational data banks, class offerings within abbreviated time periods, countless books with themes from leadership training to personal traumas, and how-to sections in Christian bookstores filled to overflowing.

148

Is it because "playing fields" are not available?—No, our communities are filled with more people to be reached for Christ than ever before, and the opportunity to build churches throughout the world is unlimited. If there has ever been a time when Jesus' words, "Lift up your eyes, and look on the fields; for they are white already to harvest" (John 4:35), are appropriate, it is today.

Is it because the talent pool of players is at a low ebb, and no one wants to play the game?—No, there are more believers alive today than ever in the history of Christendom; and like today's modern athletes, they can run faster and longer, jump higher, and execute more intricate plays than ever before.

New coaches are often quoted in their initial interviews as to the importance of building a system which will ultimately produce a winner. They are making a point that this approach, though it may require time, is worth the effort. Shortcuts will never build a great team. Systemic thinking helps one to see the big picture. Every part is important but must be understood in relationship to the entire process. Every player must understand his or her assignment and understand how it blends with the efforts of other team members.

With the dilemma on my mind of why we don't have more growing Sunday Schools, I picked up the flight magazine and flipped through the pages. My eyes were drawn to an article about building a winning system in the airline industry:

"An airline is an extraordinarily complex business. Thousands of factors affect

"When your work speaks for itself, don't interrupt."
—Henry J. Kaiser

149

The church is blessed with the brightest, most articulate leaders ever.

every aspect of the operations, every minute of the day. Keeping track of it all, and maintaining control while facilitating the safe, ontime completion of every flight, is the task of Systems Operations Control, which we call SOC."

SOC monitors the daily progress of 4,150 flights—about one departure every 20 seconds. "SOC's job is never routine. Every time something unexpected happens—whether it is air-traffic backup, a weather delay, a mechanical problem, a computer outage, an earthquake or volcano, a watermain break, a security incident—SOC's experts go into high gear, calling on years of experience and sophisticated decision-support tools to evaluate all the options and act quickly and decisively to minimize disruptions, while ensuring the safety of our customers, our people, and our aircraft and facilities.

"There is lots of gee-whiz gadgetry involved in all this, but the key to making it all work is good-old-fashioned teamwork. People from all disciplines routinely interact to solve problems.

"As you sit back and enjoy your flight today, you can be sure that SOC is doing everything possible to keep your trip running safely and on time."[1]

As I traveled through a mass of thunderheads that afternoon, I felt a sense of calmness because of the functioning system of expertise and skills.

Effective Bible Teaching-Reaching Ministries require building systems which work under all circumstances. Every part is important but must be understood in relationship to the entire process. Careful attention to these matters

150

is what builds a winning team.

Southern Baptists are indebted to Gene Mims, vice-president of the Church Growth Group of the Sunday School Board for writing a book that encourages churches to become more effective in ministry and in choosing the church's main efforts in ministry—a book that encourage churches to be involved in endeavors which make a difference to the kingdom of God. *Kingdom Principles for Church Growth* stated succinctly this objective.[2]

Kingdom Principles for Church Growth identifies the Great Commission as the foundation of everything the church is to do. Out of the mandates of the Great Commission flow five functions: worship, discipleship, evangelism, fellowship, and ministry. A church which consistently involves itself in these five functions, while being obedient to the Lord's Great Command, will also reap four wonderful results: spiritual growth, numerical growth, ministries expansion, and missions advance.[3] Mims' 1-5-4 Principle was created as a result of discussions and finally, a written document, which connected biblical teaching to practical, everyday, Christian ministry.

Gene Mims and Mike Miller, director of the Church Leadership Services Division at the Sunday School Board, produced, in 1995, the companion resource to *Kingdom Principles for Church Growth*, *Kingdom Principles Growth Strategies*, a practical resources which assists churches in identifying strategic thinking and chosen actions which will enhance their efforts in the Lord's work.[4]

Does it work? The new vitality in the

"Ideas are powerful things, requiring not a studious contemplation but an action, even if it is only an inner action."
—Midge Decter[5]

151

churches which have adopted this new vehicle of application and those which have instinctively performed the 1-5-4 principles, even though they did not have knowledge of the process, give strongest testimony to its value.

One Saturday morning in March 1995, I received a copy of an email message which Rick Warren, pastor of the Saddleback Church in Mission Viejo, California, had sent to Gene Mims at the Sunday School Board.

Out of the mandates of the Great Commission flow five functions: worship, discipleship, evangelism, fellowship, and ministry.

Bill,

I just wanted you to see this message I sent to Gene Mims.

Gene,

I want to ask your permission to quote you a couple of times in the book I'm writing.

After 15 years of teaching the Purpose-Driven Church seminar to over 20,000 pastors, I'm finally putting the material in print.

Anyway, what I've taught for 15 years is this: Church growth is the natural result of church health. Church health comes from balancing the five purposes of the church found in the Great Commission and the Great Commandment. Sound familiar? This book will dovetail PERFECTLY with the 1-5-4 principle and give people a WORKING MODEL of everything your book teaches. It has worked well—producing the fastest growing church ever in the history of the SBC according to research done at Liberty University. Last week we had 9,648 in worship.

If you have the time, I'd like to send you the first draft to read and, if you feel comfortable, write an endorsement. We are on the exact same wavelength.

Later, I commented to Gene Mims,

152

"That was quite a compliment regarding your book and how important it is in ministry."

Mims' response was, "I did appreciate it, especially since I have never met Rick Warren."

Servants in the Lord's work do not have to meet one another or be together to be on the same wavelength. The Spirit of God moves in hearts to bring about His purpose.

If you are coaching an athletic team, raising a family, building a business, encouraging fellow believers, or developing a great Bible study ministry, you will be more effective if you build a system on the foundation of Jesus Christ, the Chief Cornerstone in any system.

A great Bible study ministry is build on the foundation of Jesus Christ.

Personal Learning Activities

1. What actions does your church take to accomplish Flake's five steps?

2. In what ways does your church model the five functions of the Great Commission as listed in Gene Mims' 1-5-4 Principle? In what ways is your church seeing the four results indicated? What is Sunday School's role in these actions?

[1]Robert I. Crandell, "Vantage Point," *American Way*, May 1995, 8.

[2]Gene Mims, *Kingdom Principles for Church Growth* (Nashville: Convention Press, 1994).

[3]Ibid., 6.

[4]Gene Mims and Mike Miller, *Kingdom Principles Growth Strategies* (Nashville: Convention Press, 1995).

[5]Midge Decter, *The Liberated Woman and Other Americans*, pt. I, ch. 3.

153

Chapter 18
The Dreaded Q Word

"**D**aring as it is to investigate the unknown, even more so it is to question the known."

—**Kaspar**

Certain words create mental odors. Just the sound of the word brings to memory unpleasant scenes. Often particular mental images are specific to an age group or a portion of society.

- New York Mets fans dislike the word *Yankee*.
- Events have a way of changing feelings toward names such as Oswald, Hitler, Manson.
- Today, the word *Barney* can bring out an unusual amount of disgust from some parents in American society.

One word I have never liked is *quarterly*. This term *quarterly* has come to denote Bible study periodicals which are produced four times a years—hence the name *quarterly*. It even seems to sound worse when used in the plural form, *quarterlies*.

- People speak of "ordering quarterlies."
- They ask, "Did you receive your quarterly?"
- They ask, "Did you agree with the quarterly."
- They share, "I was reading in the quarterly."
- They say, "I forgot to bring my quarterly."

155

Why is it the ship beats the waves when the waves are so many and the ship is one? The reason is that the ship has a purpose.

Surely there is a better word to describe some of the finest pieces of Christian literature ever produced. Many have attempted to recast it as a study guide or simply a member book. None of these terms has been able to replace the Q word.

The Bible study guide which is provided in the average Sunday School class is probably the most important piece of curriculum available to the believer today. Few leaders have ever come to realize the potential of this resource. It has the potential to help more people understand and enjoy the reading of God's Word than any other Christian publication.

The Sunday School Board produces quality curriculum resources with these characteristics:
- Pupil centered
- Age appropriate
- Comprehensive in scope
- Applicable to life situations
- Bible based
- Doctrinally sound
- Targeted to reach the lost
- Easy to use
- Cost effective

This list is packed with informative truth. The problem with a "sound bite" list is that it often does not carry the full impact of the intended message. Just as a two-sentence response shared on the evening news may not portray the full impact of the entire speech, brief listings of facts are fraught with the same shortcomings.

The Bible study guide or member

156

book, which is provided in the average Sunday School class, is probably the most important piece of curriculum available to the believer today. Please take a moment to let that statement penetrate your thoughts.

You are probably mentally asking the following questions:

• Are you saying the member book is more important than the preparation materials provided to teachers?

• Are you implying that the member book is more critical to the learning process than the teaching procedures in leadership resources?

Yes, I am! If your congregation never bought another piece of curriculum from any source, teachers would somehow find commentary sources to help them interpret the scriptural truths they are teaching. They would also produce or secure helps in learning procedures and life application for their classes.

The member book is the most dynamic piece of curriculum available to the class, yet few leaders ever realize the potential of this resource. If they understood its far-reaching possibilities, the following would not take place:

• Member books are often found in closets or cabinets, having never been distributed to the members.

• Little or no instructions are ever provided to class members about how they might use this learning resource to increase their understanding the Word of God.

• When it is used, many times the member book is used incorrectly, generating a message that the Bible is not the primary focus in the class. For example, an unprepared teacher reads

The Bible study guide or member book, which is provided in the average Sunday School class, is probably the most important piece of curriculum available to the believer today.

157

Sunday School dated curriculum has the potential to help more people understand and apply the reading of God's Word than any other Christian publication.

to class members from the study guide rather than the Bible.

• Leaders fail to provide study guides for the members, reasoning that the teacher is the only one who needs supplementary help.

The member book or study guide has the potential to help more people understand and apply the reading of God's Word than any other Christian publication. Let me clarify my thoughts concerning the member study guides produced by the Bible Teaching-Reaching Division of the Sunday School Board.

1. The member study guide is the only companion piece the average layperson has besides the Bible. Teachers often have commentaries, Bible atlases, and additional helps.

2. The member study guide provides an insightful commentary for further biblical studies.

3. The member study guide has more material dedicated to application of Christian values than any other publication.

4. The member study guide is the constant monitor of doctrine. Trained biblical scholars provide insightful commentary, designed to assist the reader in examining the truths and teachings of the Word of God. It is read and reread by many sources prior to publication. Strict attention is given to correct interpretation of Scripture, both in commentary and in life application.

Why is this point so important in today's churches?

• Few periods of history have been bombarded with as many varieties of false teachings as today. Bookstores of every ilk are located in

158

malls and shopping centers. Believers can innocently be drawn into these environments and come into contact with materials and teachings which often seem in harmony with the Bible but are, in reality, a dark departure from the truth.

A pastor recently told me that one of his teachers eagerly shared her excitement about a book she had bought in a local mall bookstore and that she had purchased 25 copies to give to her class. The pastor was shocked when he heard the title, for it represented one of the leading sellers in the New Age movement. The teacher was not trying to undermine the truths of the Scripture, nor was she trying to share heretical readings with her class. She was just uninformed as to what she had innocently selected.

The member study guide is the most important piece of curriculum available to the believer today.

• Many churches have almost abandoned leadership training for their faculty members. Teachers are left alone to furrow out the truths of the Word of God. Without proper leadership, teachers may innocently propose certain tenets which can be detrimental to the accurate teaching of biblical truths.

Regardless of teacher orientation or bias, the member book provides a true compass north on biblical doctrines. Pastors and church leaders can benefit from the use of this tool which can work consistently to build up the body of Christ.

5. The member study guide provides educational materials about missions, polity, and denominational emphases.

6. The member study guide includes resources which encourage members to conduct their own weekday Bible study classes. Almost four mil-

159

The possibilities for involving people in Bible study groups are unlimited.

lion people attend Bible study every week in Southern Baptist Sunday Schools. The possibilities for involving people in Bible study groups are unlimited. The member book has simple outlines and helps which can be used by the members to involve others in Bible study.

7. The member study guide reinforces the objectives of the congregation in fulfilling the Great Commission. One of the greatest detriments to the advancement of ministry is the fact that many members either do not understand what the church seeks to accomplish or they have never bought in to the strategic plans of the membership. The member's book reinforces the overall objectives of the congregation, thereby making possible the accomplishment of goals as far-reaching as starting new classes or entering a bold new mission adventure.

8. The member study guide enables believers to be involved in an ongoing, systematic study of the Scriptures.

9. The member study guide encourages members to read the Bible and pray daily.

10. The member study guide is one of the best resources for membership visitation, especially absentees. Regardless of the attitude of the delinquent member, few ever refuse to receive the gift of an attractive member book, shared in the love of Christ. This represents another effective means of ministry which has been overlooked in recent years.

11. The member study guide is the best value available to churches. Talk today compares the value of undated curriculum as opposed to dated materials. No doubt, churches sometimes need to purchase certain materials which can be

160

taught at any time. The dangers of moving away from ongoing, dated materials include:

• The cost of undated materials often exceeds dated resources by as much as 400 percent.

• The excessive cost often encourages leaders to purchase materials only for the teacher, thereby neglecting the needs of the members. This practice is often seen when study materials are available for instructors; but only a one-page, interactive worksheet is available for the remainder of the class.

• Members fail to get a comprehensive view of Scripture when subjects taught are random.

Laypersons' need for effective Bible study has never been more acute than it is today and will be in the next millennium. Maria Martinez, vice-president of the American Bible Society, sounded the following warning in an address during Woman's Missionary Union Week at Ridgecrest Conference Center in June 1995. "Approximately 95 percent of all homes in the U.S. have more than one Bible. Yet most Bibles that are sold are given as gifts, and people tend to use the Bible as a good-luck charm. They don't necessarily value or follow its message and guidance."

Despite the potential for knowledge, Martinez noted: "There is a rising level of biblical illiteracy in the Christian community. A recent research study revealed that although 8 out of 10 persons in this country call themselves Christians, half of those don't know that Jesus preached the Sermon on the Mount. Americans say that they believe the Ten Commandments, but they can't name them. And some Christians who are in church on Easter Sunday don't know

The member book is the best value available to churches for ongoing Bible study.

161

The Bible Teaching-Reaching Division of the Sunday School Board offers quality Bible curriculum resources for leaders and members of all ages.

what they are commemorating."

This erosion of biblical knowledge among Christians results in the loss of a personal witness, she said. "We [Christians] are responsible for sharing the Christian message with others. Yet a solid, biblical foundation is too often absent from our minds and hearts. And, regrettably, too often the difference between our words and actions is great."

Bible study leaders will find many benefits from using Christian curriculum in the 21st century. The dreaded Q word can be replaced with another Q word—*Quality* Bible study resources.

Personal Learning Activities

1. Develop your own list of benefits for using dated curriculum. Share the list in a weekly planning meeting and ask teachers to add to the list.

2. Evaluate the line of curriculum used in light of these benefits. Add to the list benefits of using your chosen curriculum line. Include the ways it specifically meets the needs of your congregation.

162

Chapter 19

Presentation Communication

"Contrary to the views of some of its critics, effective Sunday Schools are not archaic in their methodology. No traditional organization can survive for two centuries without methodological adaptation."

—Thom Rainer[1]

I do not remember the year or the city, but I still remember the emotion I felt when I walked past the hotel conference room for a large annual meeting of religious educators. It was a vast ballroom, with enormous lights and sliding wall partitions. Chairs had been appropriately lined up for the gathering of an expected five hundred educators.

• Educators were traveling from all parts of the country to this important meeting where ideas and concepts would be eagerly discussed and implemented in the years ahead.

• Thousands of dollars would be spent by participants and leaders.

• Untold hours of preparation had been given to make sure this would be one of the finest meetings ever.

• The new president and elected officers were ready.

• Displays were set up in the hallway.

The next 15 years will be the golden years of Christian communication in the church.

• Faithful members were staffing registration booths.

• Refreshments were ordered for break times.

• Breakout rooms were assigned and clearly marked.

Yet something was wrong. Poised at center stage of this grand facility stood a lonely looking overhead projector, equipped with a weak lamp, probably purchased years earlier by an audiovisual department. A closer examination of the projector revealed a colored foil, duplicating a typed paper with font size set at 12.

This aged devise, faintly projecting an image which would probably be seen for only about five rows deep into the audience would be our key source of communication to those attending this meeting—cutting-edge practitioners of Christian education. I was excited about the possibilities of being in the company of these people whom I admired so much, but I knew something was amiss with what I saw as I gazed into this unoccupied hall.

I stayed around. Others did not.

Our society is so visually oriented, the leader or organization which does not stay up-to-date and involved in communications patterns will be passed by. My concern at the hotel conference site was that if the leading educators did not model current communication skills where would that leave the average Christian educator. It seemed to broadcast the wrong image—that Southern Baptist leaders would be dragged, kicking and screaming, into the next generation of communications.

I have often said that today and

164

tomorrow represent the most exciting times ever to be active in Christian ministry. Communities are filled with persons who hunger for the Bread of life, and many are awakening to find that secular promises of the last 30 years have proven to be empty and without purpose.

The next 15 years will be the golden years of Christian communication in the church. Technology abounds, and falling prices make possible opportunities of which educators of another generation could only dream.

The World Is Filled with Mark Brownings

I first saw him when I walked through the welcoming line for new members. He and his wife were an attractive couple, not unlike many who joined our church. Attired in casual clothing, Mark Browning was typical of the membership of the 90s—well educated, exercise oriented, and remarkably fit to deal with a variety of subjects and interests.

Mark told me that he worked for a computer company named Aldus.

I immediately responded: "I am one of your best customers. I have been using Persuasion [a software product produced by Aldus for computer and video presentations]."

Mark replied that he had been transferred to Dallas to assume the key role as research manager for Persuasion products.

Excited, I answered, "Mark, you and I are going to be good friends."

We did become friends. Mark allowed me to become a "beta user" for Version 3 of Persuasion, and he agreed to be a guest lec-

Technology abounds, and falling prices make possible opportunities of which educators of another generation could only dream.

165

The typical member of the 90s is well educated, exercise oriented, and remarkably fit to deal with a variety of subjects and interests.

turer to my seminary class which I taught as an adjunct professor.

One day he told me of an experience with the Sony Corporation. Officials at Sony had asked Mark to write the operating software for their new Bookman, a CD ROM player. Mark looked at me and said: "Bill, soon you will be able to take all of your computer and video presentations and transfer them, yourself, without professional assistance, to CD ROM. Then you can use a devise similar to Bookman to present them to groups of 25 or 25,000 any place in the world."

I was amazed. "Wow, but won't that be expensive?"

Mark countered, "By the time I finish writing the instructions for the software, probably $500."

My mind exploded with possibilities. I could see the Bible teacher of the future, walking into a classroom, with a myriad of possibilities related to presentation. He or she would be limited only by imagination and willingness to work.

Preschoolers are on the Internet nightly. Children manage more computer power than their engineer fathers commanded a few year ago. Young people use communication tools as easily as their parents sharpened a number 2 pencil. It is reported that when one discards an old birthday card, more computer power is thrown away than existed before 1948.

Our churches are filled with Mark Brownings. They will not be challenged, and in many cases they will not even grant a hearing to a generation of teachers and leaders who con-

166

duct their ministries as if they think filmstrip projectors are the latest and the greatest.

Get in Today

I led a conference on computer presentations, and a participant responded: "Bill, I am not going to learn that new stuff. I'm 59, and I won't learn it."

I thought: *You do not have a choice. If you don't get into that arena, in a brief time you will not be able to operate your own kitchen.*

Christian educators must get into the computer world, and they must become conversant with as many aspects of the process as possible. The following illustrates why I make such a strong statement.

When computer technology first arrived on the ministry scene, all were impressed at the possibilities. Lists of members could be easily generated, and work which had either taken large amounts of time or was impossible to accomplish was easily completed in minutes.

I remember how amazed I was to hear a corporate secretary tell me in 1978 that she used a typewriter with a screen that allowed her to make corrections rather than using "white out."

The problem incurred by allowing others to provide computer information for you is that you are limited by their knowledge or understanding of your needs. Computer programmers rather than Christian educators will design your programs if you do not learn, and they do not know the needs of your people or have the years of experience in your field.

The teacher of the future will be limited in presentation only by imagination and initiative.

167

Christian educators are the only ones who can ask the right questions. You will never receive the right answers as long as you are restricted to what the possibilities might be, especially if the right questions were poised as they dealt with the possibility of expanded ministry.

Don't be afraid to take a technological leap. Help is available.

Personal Learning Activities

1. In what ways is your church benefiting from the technological revolution?

2. What goals do you have for enhancing training and teaching with technology?

[1]Thom Rainer, *Giant Awakenings* (Nashville: Broadman & Holman Press, 199).

An institution may spread itself over the entire community. But the average person will almost always form a judgment of it through contacts with one individual. Each member of an organization who comes in contact with the public is an agent; and the impression made is an advertisement, which will make an indelible impression on the mind of the prospect.
—Dallas Office

168

Chapter 20
Encourage-ment for the Future

"Tomorrow is worth looking forward to when you serve the Lord."

—Dale Evans

Technology has advanced in quantum leaps during the last 15 years, and it appears that the average church leader is about to consider being a part of this revolutionary happening. Computers and communications knowledge are becoming commonplace, and new leaders are moving to the outer edge of participation.

A new language has developed which has enabled church leaders to be more effective in their strategic thinking. People talk about "demographics," and most of the names for new publications have titles such as *On-Line* and *InSync*. Cellular telephones, faxes, modems, and email are 90s vocabulary for today's church leaders.

This is a marked and encouraging difference from the leadership of the past which more often than not fought any movement toward this direction. Stories abound about preaching such as "The Devil's Black Box—the Radio" and the evils of "The One-Eyed Monster—the Television."

I have often said that the 90s and the approaching 21st century are the most exciting times ever to be a religious educator. As

169

I have seen the past, and I love the future.

I speak to seminarians across the United States, I find myself wanting to turn back the years, almost wishing that I were in their place. These coming years will be exciting and stimulating.

I am encouraged by the possibilities of technology in reaching people for Christ and the openness of this generation to use these new tools. But what causes me to be truly encouraged about the future is the next generation of leaders.

These so-called busters will be uniquely equipped to handle the vigorous pace of the next century. Growing up in the television and computer age, these leaders will take for granted mind-expanding products. They will use them as tools for effective ministry. The key to success in the 21st century will be the same as the key to the 1st and 20th centuries—God-called leaders who make a difference.

I have identified ages 24-38 as the target points of my ministry as director of the Bible Teaching-Reaching Division. I ask them to stay in touch with me. I tell them to call me if I can help them. Young seminarians often seem shocked when I take the initiative to foster this relationship. My motives stem from two sources:

• I am returning a favor because those who preceded me offered the same help to my ministry.

• The key to the future is always sharing from generation to generation.

Recently I visited Houston, Texas, on a routine, church consultation. I was also invited to speak to the congregation on a Sunday evening. I completed the assignment and afterwards traveled back to Nashville.

A week later I received the following

170

email message, sent via CompuServe, from a 17-year-old young man who had been present during the presentation. As you read his message, I think you will also be encouraged about the ability of this next generation to carry the torch of God's message into the next millennium.

> Dear Dr. Taylor:
> I cannot tell you how much I enjoyed this past Sunday evening. Your words were challenging, inspiring, and convicting. The church today has a long way to go to get back to its truest and deepest roots. But our hope is in the fact that God's grace is always ready to help us soar on the wings of His Spirit.
> Throughout the days that have passed since Sunday, I've thought about the ministries of the church, especially those in the area of Christian education—true higher learning.
> (I always seem to judge my enjoyment of a presentation based on how much wrangling and soul-searching it brings about. Many presentations offer information, but rarely do they provoke ongoing thought. When they do, God has moved and continues to move. He always speaks more clearly in revelation than in rhetoric.)
> God has filled those times of reflection in the afterglow of Sunday with many thoughts. The first I had—as I shared with you Sunday night—was that the church should be about trying to find enough classes for all its leaders rather than enough leaders for all its classes. The church confesses to a sad state when the majority of the members feel they are not yet disciples enough to obey the Great Commission and when those same people deny that God's grace is sufficient for Him to use them. My question for them is, Why have a God powerful enough to save yet too disinterested to sustain?
> Which led me to a second question: What if there

"Kids learn more from example than anything you say. I'm convinced they learn very early not to hear anything you say, but watch what you do."
—Jane Pauley

171

The key to success in the 21st century will be the same as the key to the 1st and 20th centuries—God-called leaders who make a difference.

were no adult Sunday School for one year? What if all those who filled the rolls had to find a role to fill? It would be the best year in Sunday School history! Not because the current system is ineffective. Not because it would tend to strain out the lukewarm members. It would be great because God would be working in each and every one of them.

Look at the apostles: Few if any of them would have been recruited by a minister of education. But they were recruited by God. His grace did in them and through them what they could not do in and through themselves.

Why are men like John, Peter, and Paul such heroes in our faith? Not because they were super-spiritual but because God poured the resources of His Spirit into them.

The last thought I've had has to do with the reason so few allow God to use them. Pride. Being used by God demands a confession of dependence on Him.

I have just begun reading *The Ragamuffin Gospel* by Brennan Manning. It has strong teaching on the pride of today's church in America. He convincingly argues that our pride has lost us our understanding of God's grace. We mistakenly think our efforts and energy are what move the kingdom of God.

I can't help but remember David's sin in ordering the census of the fighting men of Israel (see 1 Chron. 21). I just pray that we—like David—will quickly see our need for mercy and realize that our surrender to God demands a cost. May we only be willing to give by His grace whatever He requires of us.

I believe this past Sunday will be one of the defining moments in molding my philosophy of ministry. It served as a perfect complement to what I am learning daily as I serve as a student ministry intern. In some ways your job and my job are interlocking puzzle pieces: While you help direct the central teaching vehicle of the

172

church, I help organize and write daily quiet times, organize discipleship groups, and other things that help others to know Him. I am loving this more than anything else I have ever done!

Scott Bertrand, John 17:3

We must dare to confront our possibilities. And with young men like Scott around, I am encouraged about the future because the Lord continues to raise up leaders with a heart for the things of God. The coming generation of ministers of Jesus Christ will not only be adequate for the times, but they will excel because of His grace.

Personal Learning Activities

1. Who mentored you? In what ways did they shape your ministry or your Christianity or your work in the church?

2. Whom do you mentor? What steps can you take to ensure the church will have able leaders in the days ahead?

"The uncreative mind can spot wrong answers, but it takes a creative mind to spot wrong questions."
—Antony Jay, *Management and Machiavelli*

173

Chapter 21
Our Destination—Off the Map

"**N**ever go a certain way because others are going that way. Find your own way."

—Margaret Thatcher

Two events influenced me greatly during my first years in ministry. One was my seminary experience, and the other was a chance hearing about a sermon which was preached at an evangelism conference.

The favorite topic of conversation during my seminary training usually came up in the coffee shop between classes. Students talked about where they might serve after graduation. Some already had responsibilities on church staffs. They were the ones who constantly discussed their "situation." You could hear the following:

- "I am serving in a unique situation."
- "My situation is different."
- "If you could experience my situation, you would understand."

As these students graduated, I watched many cover the country with resumes. The seminary had a placement service which

175

If humans have the ability to build a small machine capable of beaming information to three satellites and then pinpointing any position on earth within 10 feet, surely the Lord knows where we are.

worked with churches, associations, state organizations, and Baptist agencies. The resumes helped to inform and connect potential staff members and available positions.

For many, the sending of resumes continued long into their ministerial career. Every time the "situation" became difficult, the temptation was to fire up the copy machine and start moving resumes.

The chance hearing of the topic of a sermon happened when my evangelist friend Mickey Warlick told me about hearing Landrum Leavell speak at an evangelism conference in Dallas. Leavell said: "God knows exactly where you are. He has placed you into His service. Do you believe that? Of course you do. You know that the Lord has called you to preach or serve in ministry. But, if you believe that, why are you always seeking to move? You call preacher friends. You distribute your resumes. Men of God, God knows where you are. He will give you a new place of leadership when it is time. Stay planted where God placed you!"

When I heard Leavell's admonition, I felt guilty that I had often fallen to the same disbelief regarding God's watchcare over my life and ministry. I did believe that God knew where I was and that He cared for my well being.

Global Positioning System

During the summer of 1995, I provided leadership at Glorieta and Ridgecrest for the first time in my role as director of the Bible Teaching-Reaching Division. Having the opportunity to encourage various church leaders on a nightly basis was exciting.

176

My son brought his family to Ridgecrest. One afternoon he showed me a birthday gift, given to him by his business partner. The gift was an instrument about the size of a book. It was a GPS—Global Positioning System. It communicates information and data with three satellites circling the earth. It can mark the location of an object or person anywhere on the globe with an accuracy reading within 10 feet.

My son is a sportsman and often takes his boat 10 to 50 miles off the coast of Florida. Using the GPS, he can monitor his positions in uncharted waters and then direct the boat back to safety, crossing channels, reefs, and other potential dangers.

"**Y**ou must either find a way or make one."—Hannibal

I turned on the GPS at Ridgecrest, and the following coordinates plotted my position at B. W. Spilman Auditorium, within 10 feet: 35° 37 m 25 sec N by 82° 16 m 26 sec W.

During a computer presentation that evening, I noted that if humans have the ability to build a small machine capable of beaming information to three satellites and then pinpointing my position on earth within 10 feet surely the Lord knows where we are. The congregation responded with applause.

As we face the prospects of a third millennium A.D., we need to be reminded of God's providential care and love. Regardless of what the future may hold, believers can find solace in knowing that God never misses by even 10 feet. The Word of God promises that He knows the "hairs on our head" (see Matt. 10:30). He knows exactly where we are and where He wants us to go.

177

"We have to be able to count on each other doing what we have agreed to do."
—Phil Crosby

Marching Off the Map

Legend has it that a Roman general was engaged in a mammoth conflict which forced him into unexplored territory. Dispatching a messenger back to Rome, the general made the following plea, "Send new orders, for we have marched off the map."

This illustration moves my heart. That general bravely took his troops into an unknown region. He acknowledged his plight and calmly asked for new orders.

Three truths can come from this story and the use of the acronym MAP:

Manpower.—Human resources equip and build an army of leaders.

Accountability.—Accountability implies importance. This is a great job.

Process.—Divine attention to details will provide effectiveness.

We may know little about the regions we will march into in the 21st century, but we have this assurance:

• We know with certainty that we will have no need for additional orders. The Great Commission and the Word of God are sufficient for whatever may come our way.

• We are not alone on this safari of faith into regions of darkness and uncertainty. Even if the Roman general received additional orders, the commander-in-chief of the Roman Empire did not join the ranks of the lost general to help him explore new lands or fight the battle. Our leader has promised us, "Lo, I am with you alway, even unto the end of the world" (Matt. 28:20).

During my preparation for writing this book, I visited the Dargan Memorial Library

178

at the Sunday School Board. I found the small book *The Organized Sunday School: A Working Manual for Officers* written by J. W. Axtell and published by Cumberland Press in 1902.

The author made his purpose clear in the introduction: "This little book is meant to be intensely practical and wholly practicable. . . . There is not in it all an atom of untested theory. . . . If in some measure the needs of a fellow worker here and there should thus be met, it will be a richly requited labor of love."[1]

Axtell commented in the first chapter: "'But,' says some one, 'the Sunday school is the Lord's work, and He will take care of it.' Certainly, he will take just as good care of it as we will make it possible for him to take; but he will not reward conspicuous laziness on the part of leaders, any more than he will reward manifest and persistent indifference on the part of the church membership. He will *not* substitute anything for official listlessness. He will *not* make our lack of method and system accomplish what method and system alone, even with his blessing, can be made to accomplish. His blessing awaits the manifestation of diligence in business—his business—the King's business.'"[2]

One chapter is given to the homework of the Sunday School director. The last paragraph is worthy of our attention: "The crown of the superintendent's homework, however, is meditation. The digestive mental process by which his school and all its interests are brought to pass and repass before him is perhaps productive of more good to his work than all his special activities put together. The quiet, undisturbed, seemingly idle hour in which his loved

"God knows exactly where you are. He has placed you into His service."
—Landrum Leavell

179

A Sunday School leader's most important time each week is the time spent in prayer for the Sunday School.

school is the subject of his thoughts is the most fruitful hour of the week. It is a time of comparison, analysis, sifting and weighing; a time of profitable retrospect; a time of taking stock of the future; a time when a solution of the trouble with that unruly class over there comes to him as an inspiration; a time when an entry into some forbidding life is clearly opened; a time when an insight into the spiritual needs of the school is revealed; *the* time of all his hours of service. Were the home the scene of no other part of the superintendent's Sunday school life except his meditation on Sunday school interests it would still be his most important field of work."[3]

I have taught for many years that one of the greatest privileges one may have is to be called to be a teacher of God's Word. We may have a paperless society in the future. We may even wear computers. But one thing is clear, if the Lord tarries: Christians will be gathering together, and someone will teach the Scriptures to the body of Christ.

Let's march off the map together!

Personal Learning Activities

1. Without aid of a GPS, describe your location in service to God right now.

2. Write a prayer about your vision, hopes, and fears for your role in service to God in the days ahead.

[1]J. W. Axtell, *The Organized Sunday School: A Working Manual for Officers* (Nashville, TN: The Cumberland Press, 1902), 7.

[2]Ibid., 10.

[3]Ibid., 36-37.

180

Afterword

Excellence in Ministry

> "To every man there comes in his lifetime that special
> moment when he is figuratively tapped on the shoulder
> and offered the chance to do a very special thing,
> unique to him and fitted to his talent. What a tragedy if
> that moment finds him unprepared or unqualified for
> the work which would be his finest hour."
>
> — Sir Winston Churchill

Our lives revolve around preparing for ministry, attempting to be the best we can be, to excel, to have excellence as a standard for all that we do in the Lord's service.

Jet pilots omit nothing in their preparation because their life depends on their readiness, knowing that one day they will soar into the heavens. Their preparation for that moment might mean not only the pilot's life but also the lives of those who entrust their lives to the pilot. Excellence, thus, becomes the byword of preparation.

There was a time when we talked of The Standard of Excellence to measure our Bible study ministry. Southern Baptists led the way. Historians outside the Southern Baptist Convention referred to what happened among a burgeoning group of rural people, intent on carrying out the Great Commission, as "the Baptist miracle."

Our Baptist forerunners in religious education literally blazed forth a path that seems almost unbelievable today—pioneering in training; outreach; innovation in grouping people; and, yes, even as long ago as the early 1900s, promoting small groups, a term that has become the buzzword for Bible study groups today. If you have attended a recent church growth conference, you would think *small groups* is a brand new term that has just come into the vocabulary of church leaders in the past 10 years.

181

Unfortunately, the message of excellence has often been replaced with the melody of mediocrity—proclaiming that in the long run everything will simply "work out." We are inundated with form not function, quantity not quality, illusion not substance.

What does the word excellence *mean?*—The dictionary calls it "the state, quality, or condition of excelling; superiority. Something in which a person or thing excels. Of the highest and finest quality; exceptionally good of its kind; surpassing superior."

How is excellence recognized?—Individuals, not organizations, create excellence. Excellence does not happen miraculously. It springs from pace-setting levels of personal effectiveness and efficiency.

- Mozart created it.
- Da Vinci demonstrated it.
- Lombardi inspired it.
- Jesse Owens performed it.
- The Nobel Prize rewards it.
- The Bible extols it.

The Bible is full of encouragement for people to excel, affirmations that God expects excellence, and instructions about our motivation to excel.

"A voice came to him from the excellent glory: This is my beloved Son, in whom I am well pleased" (2 Pet.1:17).

"Sing to the Lord, for He has done excellent things. This is known in all the earth" (Isa. 12:5).

"As for the Almighty, we cannot find Him; He is excellent in power, in judgement and abundant justice. He does not oppress" (Job 37:23).

"Do you see a man who excels in his work. He will stand before kings. He will not stand before obscure or unknown men" (Prov. 22:29).

"Let it be for the edification of the church that you seek to excel" (I Cor. 14:12).

182

Near the end of his first NFL training camp, Steve Largent found out that he was half as good as he thought he was. Cut soon after the Houston Oilers' fourth exhibition game in 1976, the fourth-round draft pick was traded to Seattle days later for an eighth-round pick. But Largent's stock went up in his years with the Seahawks, to the point where he joined Tampa Bay defensive end Lee Roy Selmon, San Diego tight end Kellen Winslow, team administrator Jim Finks, and Green Bay Packers defensive tackle Henry Jordan in the Pro Football Hall of Fame.

Largent, now a U.S. Representative from Oklahoma, headed home after being cut. He and his wife, Terry, packed everything they owned into a 4-by-6 trailer and jumped into their Ford Pinto station wagon.

"We were preparing for the rest of our life when I got the call from Seattle," Largent said.

Largent ended up catching 819 passes for 13,089 yards and 100 touchdowns—all records when he retired in 1989. He also strung together 177 games with at least one catch.

Just as Largent modeled excellence on the football field, we are called to model excellence in Christian education. Max Lucado summed it up well: "The desire for excellence is a gift of God, much needed in our society. It is characterized by a respect for quality and a yearning to use God's gifts in a way that pleases him."

Teaching Procedures

These teaching procedures have been written to lead a conference of five hours. If you are teaching a conference of a different time structure, adjust the procedures to fit your needs.

Foreword, Introductions, Preface
(5 minutes)

1. Lead participants to share what truths, traditions, and trends they have seen in their churches throughout the years (2 minutes).

2. Lead participants to thumb through the book and look at the three icons. Use a mini-lecture to help participants understand the icons: candle—traditions; torch—truth; and laser—trends (3 minutes).

Chapter 1
(7 minutes)

1. Use a mini-lecture to illustrate ways the Sunday School is "the great missionary to the future" (2 minutes).

2. Brainstorm ways to complete the sentence, "Happiness is. . . ." (5 minutes).

Chapter 2
(20 minutes)

1. Ask for individual testimonies from participants about personal mentors for Christian leadership (5 minutes).

2. Divide participants into groups of three. Ask each group to use markers and tear sheets to illustrate how the Sunday School is the "church organized" and compare experiences of their Sunday School to Bill Taylor's list of what happens when the Sunday School is the "church organized" (15 minutes).

Chapter 3
(25 minutes)

1. Brainstorm ways the hand of God has been on the life and work of the Sunday School movement (5 minutes).

2. Distribute 8 1/2 by 11-inch

184

sheets of paper. Ask participants to write newspaper articles indicating what the Bible says concerning instructions and opportunities for learning (5 minutes).

3. Use a mini-lecture to focus on Jewish history and the study of the Word of God (5 minutes).

4. Place these names and events on three-by-five-inch cards:

- Robert Raikes
- John Wesley
- William Elliott
- Steve Paxson
- B. W. Spilman
- First Sunday School in America
- First national convention
- First adult Sunday School department

Divide participants into groups of four. Assign a card to each group. Ask the group to illustrate how the person or event on their card has been a part of the Sunday School movement (10 minutes).

Chapter 4
(5 minutes)

1. Use a mini-lecture to contrast and compare the Sunday School work of Arthur Flake and J. N. Barnette (5 minutes).

Chapter 5
(10 minutes)

1. Distribute sheets of paper. Ask participants to write a letter to non-Christians telling them about Jesus' strategy of ministry (5 minutes).

2. Ask volunteers to share the importance of Bible teaching in the ministry of their churches (5 minutes).

Chapter 6
(25 minutes)

1. Divide into groups of two. Ask each person to share with the other the characteristics of the Bible teacher who has meant the most to them during their lives (10 minutes).

2. Ask participants to list ways teacher training is being provided in their churches (5 minutes).

3. Use PowerPoint or an overhead projection to place these statements before the group:

- "To a learner, everyone is a teacher."
- There are two reasons most teacher training programs do not work: BT-R administrators are intimidated by advanced teachers, and there is a feeling that the champion teacher would not benefit from attending a teacher training meeting.

185

Lead the group to evaluate and share their thoughts about these statements (10 minutes).

Chapter 7
(10 minutes)
1. Project these statements:
• List the fears of weekly planning meetings.
• List ways these fears can be overcome.
• List keys to success of weekly planning meetings.

Divide into groups of four. Ask each group to use butcher paper and markers to make these lists. Randomly select groups to share the lists (10 minutes).

Chapter 8
(20 minutes)
1. Brainstorm in popcorn fashion weaknesses in Christian education today (10 minutes).
2. Distribute sheets of paper with these individual assignments:
• Evaluate Bible teaching in your church. (Use numbers 1-10; 1 is weak, and 10 is strong).
• List weaknesses in Bible teaching in your church.
• List ways Bible teaching in your church can be strengthened (10 minutes).

Chapter 9
(15 minutes)
1. Divide participants into two groups with an assignment for each group. Provide markers, large sheets of paper, and 8 1/2 x 11-inch paper for each group to complete these assignments:
• Group 1: Write and present a TV newscast report on what "seeing the multitudes" meant in the ministry of Jesus.

Group 2: Write and present a TV newscast report about how Christians today can "see the multitudes" and minister in the name of Jesus.

Allow the groups 10 minutes to complete the assignment and two and a half minutes each to present their work to the total group (15 minutes).

Chapter 10
(8 minutes)
1. Use a mini-lecture to define *paradigm* (3 minutes).
2. Brainstorm ways churches today must move paradigms to enter the next century (2 minutes).
3. Lead participants to share ways churches must change their ministries to move into the next century (3 minutes).

186

**Chapter 11
(25 minutes)**

1. Use Powerpoint or overhead projection to highlight basic truths of how the Sunday School movement has been guided by laity (5 minutes).

2. Write the tasks of the Sunday School director on individual three-by-five-inch cards:

• Leads in spiritual accountability.

• Keeps the Sunday School focused.

• Promotes outreach and caring ministries.

• Coordinates leader recruiting.

• Encourages creation of new Bible teach

ing reaching units.

• Focuses on enlarging the Bible Teaching-Reaching organization.

• Promotes leader training and development.

Divide participants into seven groups. Ask each group to take a card, evaluate the statement, and list resources to help the Sunday School director do these tasks.

Give the groups eight minutes to complete the assignments and one minute each to report to the total group (15 minutes).

3. Use a mini-lecture to compare Sunday School leadership responsibilities of the minister of education to the tasks of the Sunday School director (5 minutes).

**Chapter 12
(10 minutes)**

1. Project this statement: "The Employment Agency of the Church." Ask participants to share how this relates to their Sunday School (5 minutes).

2. Use a mini-lecture to highlight Bill Taylor's comments about the Sunday School as "the employment agency of the church" (5 minutes).

**Chapter 13
(10 minutes)**

1. Ask volunteers to share how God has been an "ever present help for them" throughout their lives (5 minutes).

2. Brainstorm ways this truth relates to the ministries of Sunday School (5 minutes).

**Chapter 14
(15 minutes)**

1. Enlist a person who has knowledge of computers, email, PowerPoint, CD ROM, and so forth to share how these tech-

nologies can relate to Bible Teaching Reaching-Ministry (10 minutes).

2. Challenge participants to list ways modern and future technologies can help us to be Christian mentors (5 minutes).

Chapter 15
(5 minutes)
1. Brainstorm ways Sunday School is patterned after the ministry of Jesus (2 minutes).

2. Use a mini-lecture to relate the list to ways the ministry of Sunday School lends itself to church growth (3 minutes).

Chapter 16
(15 minutes)
1. Develop a lecture and project major points to define when a church is innovative (15 minutes).

Chapter 17
(10 minutes)
1. Prepare and distribute photocopied sheets with these questions:

• What steps does your church take to accomplish Flake's Formula?

Know the possibilities.

Enlist, train, and motivate workers.

Enlarge the organization.

Provide space.

Visit in the name of the Lord.

• What role does the Sunday School in your church play in leading your church to fulfill the Great Commission?

Ask volunteers to share their answers (10 minutes).

Chapter 18
(15 minutes)
1. Brainstorm qualities of the Sunday School curriculum produced by the Sunday School Board (5 minutes).

2. Use a mini-lecture to discuss Bill Taylor's thoughts concerning the Q word (5 minutes).

3. Lead participants to list strengths and weaknesses of the Sunday School curriculum used in their churches (5 minutes).

Chapter 19
(15 minutes)
1. Project this term: "Technologies Revolution." Ask volunteers to share what this term means to them. Ask participants to share what this term means to the church today and in the future (7 minutes).

2. Distribute sheets of paper. Ask participants to make personal goals for strengthening technolo-

gy in the Bible Teaching-Reaching Ministry of their church (8 minutes).

**Chapter 20
(10 minutes)**

1. Use popcorn-style brainstorming to list qualities of personal mentors. Lead participants to share ways this book and conference can help them to be mentors for Christian leaders of tomorrow (10 minutes).

**Chapter 21
(20 minutes)**

1. Use a lecture to share what GPS (Global Positioning System) and MAP (Manpower Accountability Process) can mean to Christian education for the 21st century (15 minutes).

2. Divide participants into groups of two. Ask each person to share with the other their vision, hope, and fears in their Christian education leadership roles for today and into the 21st century (3 minutes).

3. Conclude with prayer, asking God to guide as the participants propel their Sunday Schools into the 21st century (2 minutes).

Christian Growth Study Plan
Preparing Christians to Grow

In the **Christian Growth Study Plan (formerly Church Study Course),** this book, *21 Truths, Traditions, & Trends*, is a resource for course credit in the General Church Leadership Diploma Plan and the Understanding the Basic Church Ministries Diploma Plan. To receive credit, read the book, complete the learning activities, show your work to your pastor, a staff member or church leader, then complete the form below.

  Send this completed page to the Christian Growth Study Plan Office, 127 Ninth Avenue, North, MSN 117, Nashville, TN 37234-0117. This page may be duplicated.

  For information about the Christian Growth Study Plan, refer to the current *Christian Growth Study Plan Catalog*. Your church office may have a copy. If not, request a free copy from the Christian Growth Study Plan Office (615/251-2525).

Please check the appropriate box indicating the ministry you serve in through your church. You may check more than one. You will receive course credit toward the diploma designed for your position(s).

___ **Sunday School (LS-XXX)**   ___ **Pastor and Church Staff (LS-XXX)**

COURSE CREDIT INFORMATION

Social Security Number	Personal CGSP Number*	Date of Birth

PARTICIPANT INFORMATION

Name (First, MI, Last) __ Mr. __ Miss. __ Mrs.

Address (Street, Route, or P.O. Box) City, State

Zip Code

CHURCH INFORMATION

Church Name

Address (Street, Route, or P.O. Box) City, State

Zip Code

CHANGE REQUEST ONLY

Former Name

Former Address   Zip Code

Former Church   Zip Code

*New participants are requested but not required to give SS# and date of birth. Existing participants, please give CGSP# when using SS# for the first time. Thereafter, only one ID# is required.

191